# THE LAND THAT WE DREAM OF . . .

# the
# land
# that
# we
# dream
# of...

**A PARTICIPATORY
STUDY OF
COMMUNITY-BASED
LITERACY**

**ELAINE GABER-KATZ
GLADYS M. WATSON**

Research in Education Series/19
OISE Press/The Ontario Institute for Studies in Education

The Ontario Institute for Studies in Education has three prime funtions: to conduct programs of graduate study in education, to undertake research in education, and to assist in the implementation of the findings of educational studies.

The Institute is a college chartered by an Act of the Ontario Legislature in 1965. It is affiliated with the University of Toronto for graduate studies purposes.

The publications program of the Institute has been established to make available information and materials arising from studies in education, to foster the spirit of critical inquiry, and to provide a forum for the exchange of ideas about education. The opinions expressed should be viewed as those of the contributors.

**Canadian Cataloguing in Publication Data**

Gaber-Katz, Elaine
    The land that we dream of-: a participatory study of community-based literacy

(Research in education series ; 19)
ISBN 0-7744-0361-6

1. Literacy – Ontario – Toronto Metropolitan Area – Case studies.
I. Watson, Gladys M. II. Title. III. Series.

LC154.9.T6C3 1991     374'.012'09713541     C91-093087-2

ISBN 0-7744-0361-6
Printed in Canada
1 2 3 4 5 AP 59 49 39 29 19

Editing: Ann Decter
Copy editing: IS Five Printing & Graphics/Karen Miller

Book design: Counterpunch/Linda Gustafson & David Vereschagin
Photos: ArtWork/Margie Bruun-Meyer and Stephanie Martin; Darek Banasik/Canadian Living Magazine; and from research documentation

Cover and text illustrations: Dawn Lee

Project assistant: Barbara MacKellar

To all who have helped me learn in different ways, especially my parents, John and Muriel Smith.

Gladys

For my mother, Bella Sharpe Gaber

You taught me how to be a literacy practitioner. For years I watched you in the Swank Shop helping customers to write letters, fill in forms, and read their leases. You treated everyone with a tremendous amount of respect and in a myriad of ways told each and every person that they were important and capable.

Bella, I miss your wisdom and beauty every day.

Elaine

# CONTENTS

CONTENTS

The authors of this study have produced a valuable case report on the state of the art in community-based literacy education. Focusing on three programs in Metropolitan Toronto, they have gathered data from and about learners, volunteers, staff, and governing boards. Extensive quotations from all of these sources enliven the work and provide a compelling quality of realism not generally found in evaluative studies.

The non-traditional and, to some, unorthodox approaches that characterize community-based literacy education are also responsible for the methodology employed in this study. The method used was a form of participatory research that relied heavily on interviews and observation rather than on the more common tests and measurements of formal research. Participatory research encourages reflection and self-criticism among those involved and provides the programs themselves with information useful to their ongoing development. Thus, in addition to adding important stimulus to the public discussion of community-based literacy education, this research intervention has utility for those who were its objects.

Rather than the researchers applying their own meaning to the three terms that they have indicated as central to community-based literacy education, they probed continually to discover how the programs understood the meaning of:

- learner-centredness,
- literacy from a critical perspective,
- community-building,

with the result that they uncovered significant differences among people employing the same vocabulary as well as certain contradictions between practice and theory within and among the programs.

The text contains many questions with which the authors and the programs are struggling as the practice and theory of community-based literacy education evolves. This is not a set of guidelines for those who initiate programs. It is, rather, a frank presentation of the experience of three programs searching continually for new ways to be relevant to diverse populations in varied settings.

Community-based literacy education has, in a sense, become a movement of educators who are uncomfortable with the heavy emphasis on the transmission of knowledge and skills from those who supposedly possess them to those who do not. Working largely with adults who are marginalized and oppressed within the dominant Anglo, consumer society, these educators seek approaches and content that reflect the needs and aspirations of women, immigrants, Native peoples, the poor – all who have, for whatever reason, been overlooked by the major institutions, including educational systems.

Community-based literacy education demonstrates how difficult it is to integrate, within the same program, activities and concepts associated with community development and the more traditional tasks of teaching and learning. Community-based literacy education is a hybrid – it is neither pure instruction nor pure social action. As such, it does not fit well in any one agency's responsibility or budget. Among the results of this broad focus is the fact that funding from educational agencies cannot be used to cover many informal activities essential to the community-building components of the program. Staff must either spend endless hours of unpaid time working with learners outside the classroom setting or neglect the informal, participatory involvement that enables learners to move from fear and failure to self-confidence and community leadership.

It might be easier – especially for policy-makers and funders who like problems with clear solutions – if programs were able to define themselves as one thing or the other. There are programs that do this. Taking advantage of the current interest in literacy, they focus on the teaching of reading and writing. Community-based literacy educators have consistently embraced the complexity of the issues represented in the lives of the learners and in their communities. They oppose the notion that small advances in reading and writing by themselves can change very much in the lives of those who have the least access to the legitimate rights of citizens in a democracy.

This study reveals a host of unanswered questions and invites participation in the ongoing debate over how advanced industrialized countries can ensure that those who are now left out of the benefits and privileges of society can make their voices and their experiences heard in the search for solutions. The integration of social goals with education is an effort to go beyond passive compliance with the information and messages generated by the society to the empowerment of learners for creative action for change.

The study invites readers to join the search for new ways of seeing and responding to the challenge.

Carman St. John Hunter
NEW YORK
OCTOBER 1990

# PREFACE

We may permit ourselves a certain guarded optimism about adult literacy work in Canada: in many areas there are more learners and programs than ever before, and public awareness about the issue is growing. In large measure, the credit for this is due to the learners, volunteers and practitioners, and their supporters who have taken the issue to governments and the public, secured funding, and constructed networks in support of advocacy, methods, materials, and philosophies.

To properly appreciate this recent progress, we must view it against the backdrop of literacy work in Canada as an historically undervalued adult education activity. Literacy programming has survived on the fringes of the education establishment – and often independent of it – in a variety of contexts.

In the face of challenges imposed by these contexts, literacy workers have adopted and developed a range of distinct philosophies and practices to guide their work. Five broad examples in Canada come to mind:

- voluntary literacy councils usually associated with the Laubach method;
- institution-based programs carried on by school boards, libraries, and community colleges;
- social movement-based literacy projects exemplified by

the work of various grassroots organizations, such as
those in Quebec;

- ◆ workplace literacy programs run by community and
  labour groups;
- ◆ community-based literacy programs, a relatively new
  approach, carried on mostly by small, independent
  organizations in close connection to the communities
  in which they are located.

We feel that each of these approaches deserves careful study for
its respective contributions and limitations. Literacy workers, learners, and volunteers can glean valuable information from one
another.

The conceptualization of this book occurred in 1984, a time when
adult literacy issues received very little public or government recognition and, consequently, funding was even more scarce than it is
now. The Participatory Research Group (PRG) had been active in the
literacy field for several years on a project-by-project basis, creating
materials and teaching popular education courses. As an active
member of the Metro Toronto Movement for Literacy (MTML) and a
staff person at PRG, Jenny Horsman invited a group of people
involved in literacy work to meet and discuss how PRG could build a
program that would provide on-going support for the development
of innovative work in the literacy field. Out of this, a committee was
formed.

We realized that although the term community-based literacy
described a certain type of literacy work, a more detailed description
of the practice was needed. People interested in developing an innovative and viable community-based program would require guidance.
In response to this need, we decided we did not want to provide a
model, but to illustrate the diversity and richness of community-
based literacy in Ontario. We realized the irony of publishing a model,
when a key ingredient of community-based literacy is that it evolves
differently in each community. We wanted to provide a tool that

would allow each community to invent its own creative program.

In the end, the committee developed a plan to provide a critical forum to document what was happening in community-based literacy programs. We needed to separate the rhetoric from the practice. Such terms as empowerment, learner-centred, and social change were the rhetoric, but too often, crisis management and pedagogical grappling in the dark were the practice. Since government funding has become available, government bodies and others have begun to use terminology from community-based literacy, sometimes with a different meaning. There is a concern that the terminology of community-based literacy has been co-opted. We wanted to explore our meanings of the terms that are central to community-based literacy and to provide the basis for creating a new language for the field. As well, we wanted to begin to ease out of crisis management and into a self-conscious process of community-based education and critical pedagogy.

Our committee developed a proposal and began to solicit funding. We were passed from ministry to ministry and approached one foundation after another. The Maytree Foundation agreed to provide a small amount of the funding, but we found that govern-ment departments were busy deciding which jurisdiction was responsible for literacy. After the Community Literacy Unit in the Ontario Ministry of Citizenship and Culture was formed, we finally received funding for the project. Our committee then became the Project Working Group.

In 1987, Elaine Gaber-Katz and Gladys Watson agreed to conduct the research for the project. They launched the process with research meetings in three community-based programs in greater Metropolitan Toronto. Then, having reviewed massive piles of transcribed material from the research meetings, they arranged a retreat to bring us all together – members of each of the three programs, along with the working group – to develop the analysis further. After that, Elaine and Gladys were absorbed in the long process of analysis, writing, and re-writing that produced the study that you are now reading – a study that contains the collective voice of the literacy community in greater Metropolitan Toronto, as well as a rigorous analysis by the researchers.

During the course of the project, sponsorship of the project shifted to the Ontario Literacy Coalition. The members of the project working group have remained constant, but our involvement in community-based literacy has changed and developed. Two of us were literacy workers when the project began but are now employed by literacy-networking organizations, working to strengthen the infrastructure of the literacy movement. The third member, who was initially working as a literacy researcher, continues research work but is also working in a community-based literacy program. Just as the shape of this working group has shifted, so has the shape of the community-based literacy movement. The term movement is perhaps more appropriate now than it was at the start of this project, as more progress and gains are being achieved. The infrastructure of the literacy movement in general has enabled people involved in community-based literacy to gather together and show themselves as a coherent and cohesive group, willing to examine and communicate their experience within their communities of learning. This book is one of the first proclamations of that experience; voices are raised here in concert and conflict, in search of a vision for community-based literacy.

We began as administrators of the study, but as money grew short, and the true dimensions of this project loomed before us, we found that we were better defined as friendly critics. We salute Gladys and Elaine on the completion of this study, which is a timely and valuable contribution to literacy research and practice in Canada.

Harold Alden
Jenny Horsman
Tracy Westell
MEMBERS OF THE PROJECT WORKING GROUP
TORONTO, 1990

# ACKNOWLEDGEMENTS

We are grateful to the many people who have made a commitment to this project. From the very beginning, this research study has been a collective undertaking. Everyone has worked together to make this a truly participatory endeavour.

This study was originally the idea of Jenny Horsman. Jenny provided inspiration throughout, and successfully facilitated the weekend research retreat which was central to our collective process. Jenny was also responsible for bringing together the Project Working Group which became our point of reference. Working group members Harold Alden and Tracy Westell joined Jenny in managing and supervising all aspects of the project. Harold consistently offered a rigorous and insightful critique. Tracy was outstanding, especially in the latter stages, when she assumed responsibility for managing the project during the production phase.

For helping us to capture the spirit of community-based literacy, we thank the three programs which were the case studies for the project: Toronto Adult Literacy for Action Centre (ALFA), East End Literacy, and Peel Literacy Guild. They participated in an open and trusting manner. They also responded with good humour to late night calls for more information, photos, and help with last minute details. In particular, we appreciate the leadership role taken on by Tannis Atkinson, Betsy Alkenbrack, and Heather Hufton who co-ordinated their respective programs' participation in the research process, answered questions, provided detailed information, and offered ongoing comments and critique. We also appreciate the work of Sally McBeth and Michael Moore who later assumed this co-ordinating role for East End Literacy.

The research participants engaged with us in a reflective manner, building on their individual experiences of community-based literacy to develop a collective understanding. The substance of this book is theirs: it is their understanding of community-based literacy that we have tried to capture in these pages. We thank all of the participants for their involvement in this project and their ongoing commitment to community-based literacy: Tannis Atkinson, Christine Almeida, Gwen Davies, Jude Dawes, Brenda Duncombe, Donna Zwolak, Josephine Hines, and Paul Simpson from ALFA; Betsy Alkenbrack, Sally McBeth, Karen Diver, Ruth Wehlau, and Elaine Sims from East End Literacy; and Heather Hufton, Nancy Moura, Grace Scheel, Wally Ward, Elva Duff, and Trudy Reid from Peel Literacy Guild.

Our thanks to those who read our drafts and provided much needed critiques from differing contexts: Evelyn Battell who encouraged us to be clear about our Toronto bias and to acknowledge the invaluable contributions of the many people who work in other literacy settings; Arthur Bull who gently reminded us of the different ways community-based literacy occurs throughout Ontario; Tom Gaber-Katz who grounded us by asking the quantitative questions; Nancy McHardy who correctly challenged our assumptions about the field of social work; and Kathryn Zettel who assisted us to approach our analysis with creativity.

We are also grateful to Barbara MacKellar who made all the arrangements for the research retreat, worked to tight deadlines, and recorded and transcribed the many hours of research discussions; to Christopher Simpson who assisted Barbara from time to time; David Wright who provided legal advice; David Smith who did the bookkeeping during the first year of the project; and Rachel Epstein who reviewed the research retreat agenda with Jenny.

This project could not have been accomplished without the

support of our friends and families who tolerated our innumerable evening work sessions, cranky behaviour, and the way the three month project stretched into three and one-half years. Sandy Straw fed us, and read our writing when we became punchy. Haley Gaber-Katz, who was a pre-teen when this project started, grew into a full-fledged teenager by the time the project was finished. She put up with rushed dinners, and her mother working many evenings and weekends. Tom Gaber-Katz was home when Elaine wasn't, taking care of the parenting and other home responsibilities. Sandy, Haley and Tom – you were supportive throughout. We thank you and we promise never to undertake a project of this duration again.

We acknowledge, with appreciation, the finanicial support of the:

- ♦ Maytree Foundation
- ♦ Ontario Ministry of Skills Development, Community Literacy Unit
- ♦ Multiculturism and Citizenship Canada, National Literacy Secretariat.

We also thank the Participatory Research Group and the Ontario Literacy Coalition for their sponsorship of this project.

We acknowledge permission from Leo Feist, Inc. to reprint an excerpt from *Over the Rainbow* by H. Arlen and E.Y. Harburg, copyright © 1936, 1939 (renewed 1966, 1967) Metro-Goldwyn-Mayer, Inc.

ACKNOWLEDGEMENTS

# THE LAND THAT WE DREAM OF . . .

# community-based literacy in context

"Somewhere over the rainbow
Way up high
There's a land that I heard of
Once in a lullaby . . . "[1]

People everywhere have hopes and aspirations for a better life. For as many as one in five adults in Canada,[2] this better life means becoming literate – to be able to read and write, and to discover for themselves their right to participate more fully in society. As one learner[3] poignantly expresses:

> "Once I have a little confidence . . . I'll go out and see what's there. I'll go out and face the world."

This literacy learner has a sense that there is a life out there, removed from her's, and to which she aspires. Reading her words closely, one might ask how and why it is that she and many others feel apart from society. Far too frequently, a lack of literacy skills is synonymous with economic and social exclusion: men and women who have difficulty with reading and writing are more likely than others to be poor, unemployed, or underemployed. Literacy learners are told in a myriad of ways that they do not have the skills and knowledge that are needed to contribute to community life. In this book, we explore how local communities can take responsibility for developing educational programs that recognize and build on the aspirations of some adult literacy learners.

Our setting is Metropolitan Toronto, a large, densely populated urban centre located in central Canada. While there are different types of literacy programs in this area, including those offered by community colleges, boards of education, voluntary organizations, and labour unions, this book focuses on the small, independent tutoring programs that offer literacy learning opportunities to English-speaking adults. Commonly known as community-based literacy programs, these programs articulate a goal of a more inclusive and participatory society, which respects and encompasses the aspirations of those labelled illiterate. In this book, we explore the emerging nature of community-based literacy practice and theory by researching three programs: East End Literacy, Peel Literacy Guild and Toronto Adult Literacy for Action Centre (ALFA).

An examination of the accomplishments of community-based literacy programs reveals an emerging practice and theory. They are developing organically from local and community roots. This is not a situation of "theory first, then practice." Practitioners and volunteers who are committed to similar social and political perspectives are examining social movements such as progressive education, feminism, and action against poverty. From these movements, they are selecting practices that are relevant to their own day-to-day work. It appears to us that the theory of community-based literacy is developing in tandem with, and emerging from, the practice.

Programs adopt a particular practice, such as beginning with learners' experiences and publishing student writing. Subsequently, program practitioners explore why they have adopted this approach. It is from this process that a distinctive theory begins to emerge. Practitioners realize that by choosing particular practices, they are, in fact, drawing from various theories. As they learn more about the underlying theories, they begin to identify the theories that relate to their programs and use them to improve their practice. From this, community-based literacy programs are beginning to develop their own theory.

In our exploration of this emerging practice and theory, it became clear to us that programs were focusing their discussions on three areas of practice: the way in which learning is centred on the interests and life experiences of the learner; the programs' interpretation and understanding of literacy and illiteracy; and the interactive relationship between each program and its neighbouring community. We further explored, within the context of the programs, what each of these areas of practice might mean in terms of theory. We suggest that three fundamental elements significant to the development of a theory of community-based literacy arise out of the practice: **learner-centredness**, **literacy from a critical perspective**, and **community-building**.

Throughout this book, we listen to the voices of literacy learners, community volunteers, and paid literacy practitioners. Through each voice, we discover the individual experience of community-based literacy.

> "It takes a lot of courage to come to a program. I thought to myself, 'Everyone is going to know how stupid I am.' I hid my illiteracy very well. Almost too well. Now I answer the phone at the literacy centre so that learners won't have to leave a message on the answering machine. I volunteer in the office and in the library at the literacy centre."

> "I started as a volunteer. I wanted to be part of something community-based and liked the idea of working like that. I had a very positive experience with my learner. We became friends. I felt that I was

valued and really made a difference. I decided that I wanted to get paid for what I did well, so I joined another community-based program as staff."

"Before I was a staff person, I was a tutor. I became involved because someone came up to me in a No Frills store and asked me where something was because he couldn't read. That was my first exposure to the fact that literacy was an issue in Canada. Shortly after, I saw an ad in the paper which said, 'Do you want to volunteer?' I was involved with publishing at the time, and I was thinking a lot about the fact that most of our printed material comes from a really restricted point of view. I thought about how women's experiences in the world are invisible, or at least have been until quite recently. When I became involved in literacy, I started thinking about how this is especially true for people who are undereducated. Then I got involved in publishing learners' writing. The whole thing fascinated me – tutoring, the way tutors are trained, the way education is viewed. It was exciting to find that there was a different way in which education could take place."

Beginning with individual stories such as these, community-based literacy programs move from the individual narrative to the collective voice. In addition to the collective voice of learners, volunteers, and practitioners, other voices echo throughout this book. Our voice, as researchers and writers, is also heard. We organized a participatory research process through which participants discussed their literacy practice and the underlying philosophical principles that have guided their work. (A summary of the research process appears in Appendix B.) In doing so, we acted as catalysts for many lively discussions that form the basis for this book. From our perspective as community researchers and activists in the literacy community, we framed the questions and guided many of the discussions. Our approach was analytical but supportive in spirit. This collaborative process has resulted in what we hope will be the first of many publications that examine community-based literacy work.

In this book, the voices of learners, volunteers, and practitioners appear as quotations indented from the main body of the text. We have gathered these quotations from the transcripts of the research meetings, choosing those that best reflect the general nature and tone of the research discussions. Particular quotations were selected because they were wonderfully stated explanations of a theme or dilemma, phrases around which group discussions seemed to coalesce, ideas and feelings that were stated several times, or thoughts that were unusual or unique. Although we have included many verbatim quotations from the transcripts, we have, in some cases, slightly shortened quotations in order to present the voices of as many participants as possible. For the same reason, we have chosen to present some of the participants' ideas from the group discussions in a narrative fashion rather than as direct quotes. Throughout, we have tried to retain the flavour of what was said and reflect the interchange of ideas that took place. In all cases, we have endeavoured to be respectful of participants' words and true to the printed documentation provided by the programs, whether we were presenting actual quotes or giving our analysis of the data. In keeping with the participatory nature of this study, participants were given an opportunity to review the initial drafts of this book and to comment on our presentation and analysis of their research discussions. We incorporated the many comments that we received, revising the book in light of their suggestions.

While providing opinions and perspectives, participants in the research process emphasized the overwhelming need for a book that would help others to understand community-based literacy.

"Every tutor that comes into a program should have something in their hands on the issues that surround community-based literacy. Programs prepare or buy manuals on how you train tutors, how you recruit tutors, how you teach literacy, how adult literacy students learn. But what about the broader issues that tutors have to come to grips with? Where do we present our philosophical base? Why literacy? And, what is our purpose? I think we should incorporate these issues into our training and present our perspective. We would then be able to ask: Do you understand and do you share our vision? I think that we would have fewer dilemmas to cope with in the sense that others would know that we teach people both functional literacy as well as critical literacy. And we would point to our purpose, which would back us up."

This book has been written in response to that need. It is for people who are interested in adult literacy in Canada – for literacy volunteers, tutors, and practitioners, for adult educators, and for others who work in the literacy community and in social change movements. In telling the story of community-based literacy, we seek to accomplish a number of things. We want to document community-based literacy programming in three of the thirteen such programs in existence in greater Metropolitan Toronto in 1988. We want to explore and analyze the emerging practice and theory of community-based literacy to see how both are shaping literacy and adult education programming. We hope that our work will stimulate discussion that will ultimately lead to the strengthening of the community-based literacy movement. We wish to encourage the continuing development of a community-based literacy movement and foster its links with other social change movements, while exploring an educational setting in which a community increases its collective responsibility for its members.

INTRODUCTION

# elements of community-based literacy

Three elements are intrinsic to community-based literacy: **learner-centredness**, **literacy from a critical perspective**, and **community-building**. In the language of community-based literacy, these three terms are so commonplace that frequently the creativity and complexity of the practice is obscured. There is a tendency to assume that everyone who uses these terms brings the same meaning to them. When participants in the research meetings used these terms, they assumed that we would understand completely what they meant. But the richness of the research discussions led us to believe that there is a complex, and sometimes contradictory, understanding embodied in these terms. Throughout the research discussions, we tried to discover the essence of community-based literacy by examining how these three elements have been understood, practised, and experienced. In this book, we consider each of the three elements from the collective perspective of learners, volunteers, tutors, and staff, as well as our own perspective as researchers. We look at how these three elements have shaped and strengthened community-based literacy practice. We also explore some of the challenges, questions, and contradictions that arise within the programs as they strive to ground their practice in these elements.

## LEARNER-CENTREDNESS

Learner-centredness is a cornerstone of community-based literacy. It is difficult to imagine anyone describing community-based literacy without referring to learner-centredness. It encompasses a commitment to active learning: a process whereby learners will be involved in setting their own learning goals and determining their own curriculum. It guides the literacy practice by reinforcing the prominence of learners within the programs, and encouraging respect for learners' life experiences. Learner-centredness is seen as progressive, as a true alternative to teacher-centred education. Regardless of whether the learning takes place in a one-to-one situation or in small groups, the curriculum is learner-centred and is guided by the specific educational needs of each learner.

During this study, participants indicated that learner-centredness has many components. We present these components as they were identified at the research meetings, exploring how each contributes to the development of community-based literacy, and raising questions about the contradictions and tensions that are inherent in each.

Within community-based literacy programs, learner-centredness means that programs:

- listen to literacy learners and elicit stories about their lives;
- believe that everyone can learn;
- emphasize equality among learners, volunteers, and staff;
- encourage learners to become involved, both in the program and in the community;
- ensure that learning will be relevant;
- provide a range of programming options;
- assist learners in setting their own learning goals and measuring their own progress;
- ensure that learners' interests and needs determine the curriculum.

The rigorous, genuine way in which community-based literacy programs implement each of the components of learner-centredness contributes to the excitement and energy that these programs bring to adult basic education.

### Listening to Learners

In community-based literacy programs, the practice of listening to learners has resulted in the adoption of the language experience story, both as a methodology and as a basis for curriculum. Learners write stories, which are used as reading materials, and also as the basis for devising strategies to improve skills in reading and writing. This listening to, and valuing of, learners' stories has led to a growing emphasis on publishing student-written materials.

During our research, we asked learners about their experiences and how they came to participate in a literacy program. One learner told us his story – a story which echoes the sentiments of many learners in other programs. Stories like this one form the basis of the language experience method.[4]

"I started working when I was eight years old. I never had a chance. I never had a mother or father. I had to do everything for myself. I had no one to teach me. Once, I was working in Sault Ste. Marie. I only made $10 a day. I never handled a chain saw in my life. My boss came up to me and said, 'Can you handle a chain saw?' I said, 'Sure, give it to me, I'll handle it.' The first thing that I needed to do was to figure out how to start the thing.

I never learned how to read. I had to use my wits. I got the chain saw started and I did a good job. Eventually I was fired. Later on I went to a school in Elliot Lake to learn a trade. But I started drinking because I didn't care for life. If someone had come up to me and asked, 'What are you going to do – drink or learn to read?' I would have answered that I would rather have stuck to drinking. Drinking was easier.

Even though I didn't know how to read or write I still got many a job. I used to work, oh, this is going back a long ways, on a farm. I only made $135 a month. When I asked for a $5 raise they refused, so I quit. Then I worked on a garbage truck. I had to lie to them. It was the only way to get a job.

When I went to work for the City, they said I needed grade twelve. So I lied. That's how I got my job. But I do just as good a job as anybody else. We have men there with much more education than me. And I do just as good a job as they do. But if you want a job you have to lie. When they asked me if I had a high school education, I said sure I do. Today I'm making $12.45 an hour. I wouldn't be making that if I didn't lie.

You see, in my days, they never had anything like this literacy program. Here, I come and they teach me. They also tell you what's going on. They are very good at what they do. This program is the best thing that has ever happened to me."

By listening to adult literacy learners and eliciting stories about their lives, community-based literacy programs help people learn to read and write. It is considered good pedagogy to use learners' own words and experiences as the basis for the curriculum, partly because people learn to read and write more easily when they begin with their own words that express their thoughts and feelings, rather than with the grammatical components of the language. It is also considered good pedagogy to have learners begin with familiar language based on their own experiences rather than imposed language that may be unnecessarily controlled, stilted, and culturally biased. In the process of using their own words, learners affirm and validate their life experiences. The learner-centred philosophy supports such practices. It encourages the tutor to use learner-generated stories rather than workbooks; challenges the understanding that phonics instruction is the best way of teaching literacy; and supports a whole language or multi-method approach.

While literacy practitioners recognize the value of the learner-centred approach, they also struggle with some questions and contradictions. How can this approach incorporate content from a wide variety of sources to provide a well-rounded educational experience? How can practitioners, using a learner-centred philosophy, encourage learners to value the role of other learners in the learning process?

Community-based programs have taken steps to address some of these questions. Some programs encourage learners who are participating in one-to-one tutoring to consider their own individual stories in the context of wider social issues. In addition, publications on particular issues are produced by and for learners. Small groups of learners conduct research together by reading background information, conducting interviews, and taking photographs. They then discuss the issues and write down their opinions and views. The process is not an individual learning experience but part of a collaborative group process that enables every literacy learner to be an "expert" and "knowledge-producer."[5] It encompasses the life experiences of several learners, generates learning materials from and with the learners, and does this within a social context.

### Believing in Learners

Within community-based literacy, everyone, including learners, is encouraged to believe in the learners' abilities to learn. The learners' aspirations are considered first; previous labels are not starting points. Community-based literacy programs stress that literacy learners bring all kinds of strengths, skills, knowledge, and experiences to the programs. The objective of each learning session is to identify these strengths and to build on them. It does not seem to matter that learners come to community-based literacy programs having failed repeatedly in the school system or with labels that suggest how difficult it will be for them to learn. In spite of any doubts, community-based literacy programs state that every learner is capable of learning. The focus is on learning; it is not on the limits imposed by a label. In this way, community-based literacy programs encourage learners to believe in their own capabilities.

"If you go into a formal institutional program, there is nobody rooting for you. No one says, 'If you want, I'll tell you ten times a day that you can do it.' Institutions are not set up that way, but community programs are."

"One of the things that students say they've learned is that they can learn. Other learning situations they've been in have not given them that feeling at all."

The question is whether believing in learners is enough. Learner-centredness within volunteer programs means that every volunteer, tutor, and staff member needs to unlearn what society reinforces. Society wants to idealize and revere winners. Sometimes, tutors and staff, perhaps unintentionally, tend to seek those learners who will be successful. Occasionally, tutors ask for learners "who aren't slow", or they take on a learner and confine their teaching to the alphabet and the most commonly used words,[6] having unconsciously concluded that this learner can never progress to reading for meaning.[7] Some tutors become disheartened by the amount of time it takes and wonder if their learner is dyslexic, therefore needing the services of a professional.

Believing in learners appears to be a component of learner-centredness to which everyone aspires, but there are moments of doubt. While community-based literacy programs state unequivocally that everyone can learn, some people find this hard to believe wholeheartedly, given that there are learners in the programs whose reading has not substantially improved. Even learners will sometimes blame themselves, claiming "I didn't do everything I could have done" or "I didn't stick with it long enough."

When these moments of doubt arise, staff and volunteer tutors remind each other of the importance of believing in learners. They are reminded to ask themselves whether they are truly viewing their learners as successful in terms of the learners' own measures. The reinforcement of this belief in learners gives depth to learner-centredness. It builds tolerance and a respect for difference within the programs and within the communities. It challenges notions of disability, stressing instead the importance of finding the contributions that each individual makes.

Learner-Centredness

## Equality Among All

Community-based literacy programs try to challenge the balance of power which, in typical learning environments, is weighted in favour of the teacher. They recognize that learners, tutors, and staff play different roles within a community-based program, and they want these roles to be equally valued. In their mission statements, they insist that learners must be equal partners in creating the learning process. In each of the programs, this expectation of equality is discussed among learners and tutors. Through this process, learners become aware of how they can expect to be treated within the community-based literacy program.

"I am a student. It is very important for me to feel equal to the tutors, even though we are not equal in terms of how much we know. It's very important for me to feel that I am equal in order to accomplish something."

"I really love the relationship between myself and my students. I have worked with two people from the Caribbean. Then I worked with two domestic workers. The relationship that builds up is unique in my life."

"It is like having a good friend. I know now that I'm able to learn. It was just a matter of finding someone who I'm comfortable with. If it wasn't for this program I never would have continued. It has to feel like it is coming from a good friend or from somebody in the community. That's important to me."

"I know why I came. I came for one reason: to learn. And if this is the only place that can help me, then why not? The tutors can be my friends as well as people who teach me. I learn better if I'm friends with the tutor. Otherwise I would be very nervous. I'll tell you what this literacy program has done for me. It has helped me to open up and say how I really feel, instead of sitting back and saying, 'Nice day, isn't it?'"

The relationship of equals is often a stated objective of community-based literacy. This means that learners are at the centre of the learning interaction. Sometimes, though, staff and tutors influence too strongly what learners learn and how the learning takes place. Within community-based literacy, programs recognize the continual need to reinforce the principle and practice of equality.

### Learner Involvement

The goal of having learners actively involved in a variety of aspects of the program is integral to the learner-centred program. This is not only a goal in and of itself, but also a way of assisting in the learning process. As learners become involved in different ways, they acquire new skills. Some learners help out with tasks in the office; some participate in committees and special group projects; some are elected to the board of directors; and some become involved in teaching.

"The editor of the community newspaper told me about the program. It took me two months to call. But when I went to see them they were very nice. It was the way they talked to me . . . I am no longer a learner there. I go there to tutor."

Learner-Centredness

Involving learners is not a simple process. There are many skills learners must acquire in order to do committee work competently, produce a publication, or make informed decisions as a member of the board of directors. While many programs can now say that a growing number of learners are actively involved in the program, this aspect of learner-centredness is still in the formative stage.

> "If students became more involved, they could do a lot. Maybe it would take some of the pressure off staff. It would be more of a community effort. It should be organized. They could let learners know when they were needed. We could talk to tutors about how the program runs and introduce them to learners."

> "Learners want to put something back into the program as well as taking."

This aspect of learner-centredness holds tremendous potential, but increased learner involvement will require a substantial increment in funding since staff support is needed whenever there are efforts to increase learner involvement. To date, funding for this has not been forthcoming. For example, learner involvement cannot be counted as "student hours of instruction", the measure used by boards of education to calculate their funding for programs. It is also less easily described and less favourably received in funding proposals than are activities for improving reading and writing skills. Without funding, this aspect of learner-centredness relies on the dedication and commitment of staff to work many hours of unpaid overtime. For this reason, the full potential of learner involvement remains unreached.

Just as increased learner involvement requires more staff time, it also requires a greater time commitment on the part of learners. For some learners, this additional time commitment is difficult, if not impossible, to make, given the many time-consuming responsibilities in their work and family lives.

### Relevant Learning

> "Learner-centred is simply another way of saying relevant to the learner."

"Relevant to the learner" means that the learners' understanding of the world is reflected in the learning materials, because learners inform the programs about what materials encompass their day-to-day needs and interests. It means the language and form of the materials are familiar to the learners, and the content is shaped from the fabric and texture of learners' lives. Learners acknowledge that they are much more likely to improve their reading and writing skills and increase their involvement in the community if they work with materials that are relevant, rather than spend endless hours working on irrelevant, silly exercises about "Nat and Pat on the mat." To help make learning materials and methods relevant to the individual learner, programs encourage and support student writing and student publishing, and search continually for found materials of interest and importance to learners.

### Choices

Most learners come to programs with a preference for either one-to-one or group learning. Community-based programs tend to offer a choice, with the understanding that both one-to-one and small group learning can be learner-centred.

### One-to-One

One-to-one tutoring is often regarded by both learners and tutors as a setting that fosters learner-centredness.

> "This literacy program is great. It gave me a chance to have a tutor on a one-to-one basis. It was better than a classroom where you might not understand right away and you lose out. I think one-to-one is great."

> "My learner and I have been meeting for a long time. In many ways he is on his own. He brings in whatever he wants to work on. He likes to write poetry. I don't ever really feel that I am teaching him. He is at a much higher level of literacy [than some other students]. He was never motivated to work on drills. He was really more interested in creative writing."

> "In a one-to-one learning environment you don't need to take tests, if you don't want to. You are not measuring your progress against the progress of another learner, but rather against yourself. Like with any adult learning situation, you may not need someone to tell you that you have learned what you set out to learn."

> "Sometimes when I get off from work, I'm tired and I'm beat, and I don't want a lot of noise. I need time to unwind, and the one-to-one basis sort of helps me to unwind and learn as well."

Although it would seem that the one-to-one setting is the ideal environment for learner-centredness, it is not always the case.

"While learners hope that one-to-one tutoring with
an individualized curriculum that is based on their
literacy needs will be an excellent learning situation,
it doesn't always turn out that way."

"Some learners approach neither their tutors nor
staff to say that they are having difficulties with the
way the sessions are going. They may be having a
lot of trouble, but they never question their tutors'
abilities."

Some learner and tutor pairs meet outside of the literacy centre,
and the one-to-one relationship becomes quite private. It can then
become difficult for staff to assess how the learning process is taking
shape and whether or not the learning goals are being determined
by the learners.

"Sometimes we see something that's a little bit
distressing. It is with tutors who have the best of
intentions. Some tutors encourage their learners to
become dependent on them. So that even things that
the learners might otherwise have been doing for
themselves, the tutor will end up doing for the
learner. This situation contradicts the goals of our
program. This is a difficult thing to avoid. Very
difficult. I found that when I was a tutor, this was
one of the struggles."

One-to-one learning is also very labour intensive. Learners state
adamantly and persistently that they want more tutoring than once
a week for two hours.

"I would like it if the program could offer me more
than two hours a week."

Learner-Centredness

Often, community-based literacy programs cannot offer more. Even though the programs state that they meet learners' educational needs, most community-based literacy programs cannot meet the needs of learners who want a full-time program because the programs do not have sufficient funding, staff, and space.

### Small Groups

In addition to one-to-one tutoring, community-based literacy programs also organize small group learning opportunities, which are preferred by many learners.

> "When you get used to not speaking, you internalize a tremendous amount. If you participate in a group, it is a bonding experience."

Through their participation in small groups, learners discover that they are not alone, that other adults are also learning to read.

> "My worst fear was coming to this literacy program. And after I got over the initial shock of asking for help, I realized there are so many people like me. Why was I so worried that everybody was going to know?"

> "Having a reading centre where people can gather and congregate, for get-togethers, for example, gives people a feeling of belonging. It's not like the one-to-one with the tutor every week. At the centre, they see other people doing literacy and they feel that they are part of something."

Some community-based literacy programs prefer groups over one-to-one because groups not only provide learners with the opportunity to learn from each other, but also to act collectively on issues of common concern.

> "I have a bias that there is a definite advantage to working in groups over working with individuals, in terms of gathering together the thoughts and desires of people and working in a direction that is meaningful to everybody. It has much more potential for people to act together, to do things collectively, and even to identify their own interests as group interests."

Despite the stated preference for small groups, some staff and volunteers are challenged by the question of how to be learner-centred within a small group. They perceive a tension between learner-centredness and a group-centred or collective approach.

> "In my experience with teaching a small group, I have found that it is not learner-centred. You can't race around the room having everybody doing something different. You have to operate as a group. What you have to do is sit down and negotiate the curriculum with a group of people. I find it very hard. They know the program is learner-centred and they are very demanding. To them, a good teacher should be able to give them what they want 100 percent of the time. I feel inadequate. They have a right to expect me to be learner-centred but how do you do that in a group? You have to give and take in a group. If we don't have a defined curriculum, even in a skeletal way, sooner or later we are all going to burn out. Negotiating a learner-centered curriculum in a group is very hard work."

## Goal-Setting and Self-Evaluation

In a learner-centred program, learners set their own goals and measure their own progress. In lieu of assessment tests, which are frequently used by other kinds of literacy and upgrading programs, learners meet with staff and volunteers to discuss their skill levels and goals.

> "When I started here, I set a goal for myself. I tried to push myself. I set goals of where I'd like to be this time next year, and so on. Before I never used to do that, but coming to this literacy program started me pushing myself. I push myself to see if I can go through with it."

> "I set goals for myself. I bring what I don't know here to my tutor, and I make sure I know it before I leave. You get a good feeling inside when you are learning. It's really important."

Once learners have set their goals, they are then involved in measuring their own progress. Instead of taking part in ongoing testing, learners are encouraged to assess their own progress. Usually this happens every six months when learner, tutor, and staff sit down together to review the learner's accomplishments in relation to the goals that the learner earlier identified.

> "I gave myself one year. After one year exactly, I started upgrading at an evening school. If I had stayed in this program, I would have used it as a shield or like a crutch to hang on to. I don't think I would have gone on to see what else there is. That was very important to me, once I had a little confidence in myself."

ELEMENTS OF COMMUNITY-BASED LITERACY

The de-emphasis on testing is an important attribute of learner-centred practice, but it poses some challenges for community-based programs, particularly when questions are raised by funders. Does self-assessment really demonstrate whether students have learned to read and write better? While this is a difficult question, some students are very articulate and passionate about the value of self-assessment.

> "I haven't reached my goal yet. I've got a long way to go, but I'll know it when I get there. Yes, I'll know by how I can do things – things I used to have problems with. I will be able to do these things with my eyes closed. Then I'll know. I'll know."

But not all students share this perspective. Sometimes learners themselves ask to be tested. There are some learners, for example, who wish to learn how to take a grade nine qualifying exam. Does learner-centredness then mean that community-based programs prepare those learners for tests?

There is also ongoing tension acknowledged by some staff and volunteers that, while testing may help to motivate some learners, it could be detrimental to others.

> "Some learners would fall apart if they had to come and perform. Others would find it very motivating."

> "I often feel that in our programs we do not put enough pressure on our learners to produce. I am not talking about pressure to make them fail, but pressure to help them to maintain their motivation."

## Self-Determined Curriculum

In community-based literacy programs, learner-centredness means that learners' needs determine the curriculum.

> "The curriculum isn't set before the learner walks in the door."

It also means that the curriculum grows out of the interests and experiences of each learner.

> "We want our learners to go from the known to the unknown."

Building on what the learner already knows, programs develop original learning designs and materials for each new learner. Language experience stories, using a whole language approach, are central to this process.

> "To me learning to read is a process. But it is a process that should be internalized rather than imposed. While it is true that language is structured, the best way to learn is to have that structure internalized as an extension of your experience. You don't learn grammar, you just get a sense of the language."

The integration of whole language theory into self-determined curriculum has led to the development of innovative student writing and publishing programs, which produce excellent materials. These materials are sometimes distributed to a wider audience of learners.

While most agree that a self-determined curriculum is central to a learner-centred approach, concerns still arise. One concern is about the duplication of time and effort that tends to occur when new learning designs are created with each new learner. Although there are some informal opportunities to exchange curriculum ideas among programs, there are few ongoing mechanisms to share insights about good methods and materials. Each program is usually left on its own to make the best of its own resources and creativity.

A second concern is that learners may have reservations about becoming involved in creating their own curricula. They say they aren't comfortable with this kind of approach. Yet another concern arises when a learner comes into the program asking for teaching materials and approaches that she may have used previously with little success. She may want to start with grade seven grammar because she wants to feel that she can learn it. The literacy tutor may feel that beginning with grade seven grammar would be humiliating and frustrating for the learner and would result in discouragement and defeat. While, in this instance, the curriculum would probably be negotiated between learner and tutor, the question remains: does self-determined curriculum always mean providing exactly what learners request? For some literacy practitioners, it means exactly that.

> "Here, learner-centred means grade seven grammar, if and when a student asks for it."

For other literacy practitioners, a self-determined curriculum and grade seven grammar are incompatible. The security sought in conquering grade seven grammar, for a myriad of reasons, may or may not be found. And the price of seeking this security is a high one if the end result is that the learners feel that they have failed again. For other literacy practitioners, this is not an either/or situation. While practitioners may wonder if they are doing the right thing when they give learners the materials and approaches they request, some seek resolution through a process of negotiating with learners.

Other practitioners, faced with the same questions and concerns, point to the need for the development of a pre-set community-based literacy curriculum. Not surprisingly, this topic is received with considerable ambivalence. While the adoption of a pre-set community-based literacy curriculum may reduce some of the duplication of effort, it also contradicts an important aspect of the learner-centred approach. Is it possible to write a pre-set curriculum that is centred on learners' stories and experiences? Could there be such a thing as an evolving, flexible curriculum that would incorporate each learner's interests and needs while also ensuring learners' participation in its design? With regard to evaluation, while a pre-set curriculum may be more effective in providing a specific measure of the learners' progress, it may diminish the learners' participation in their own evaluation.

There is a notion that a pre-set curriculum, by its very nature, is determined according to a presupposed image of the literacy learner. If a practitioner develops a curriculum before the learner even walks in the door, it stands to reason that the learning program will be based on the practitioner's conception of who the literacy learner is and what he or she needs to learn, as opposed to being open to what the person needs and wants, helping him or her to articulate this, and responding to it.

Programs that adopt a pre-set community-based literacy curriculum will be faced with the challenge of addressing the diversity of learners. With a self-determined curriculum, learners can each identify what they want to learn and get the attention and help they need. How would a pre-determined, community-based literacy curriculum meet the needs of learners with different life experiences and backgrounds, different skills, different knowledge bases, different attitudes, and different learning styles? Because each of these differences needs to be acknowledged and affirmed, there may be no single body of content, skills, and knowledge that can be contained in a pre-set literacy curriculum.

When we consider a pre-set curriculum, there is a concern that learners' needs may not be met. With a self-determined curriculum, this may also be the case. This is because the very concept of "needs" is problematic. The discourse of literacy suggests that programs ought to work with learners' needs. But who has created the discourse: learners, volunteers, staff, or the community at large? In part, the concept of need is an outcome of service provision. It is a term commonly used by social service providers who earn their living "meeting the needs" of people who are the recipients of their services. Within community-based literacy, some of the commonly used terms come directly out of a social service model – a model that is sometimes critiqued by community-based literacy practitioners. This social service model includes terms such as needs assessment, intake, and learning contracts.

By borrowing and using these terms without critical reflection, community-based literacy programs may be missing some of the implications that result from their use. For example, who decides that learners want literacy programs that don't have a pre-set curriculum? Who designs the questions that will be posed to learners? Who manages the process? Who analyzes the data? And, what skills and knowledge do learners need in order to reflect upon their own needs? While we do not have answers to these questions, we feel that they call attention to the danger of claiming categorically that a self-determined curriculum is more desirable for literacy learners than a pre-set curriculum.

Another question, and a point of some tension, is whether a self-determined curriculum, which focuses on the individual learner's experience, can also be a "social change" curriculum that will support the empowerment of individuals and the community through collective social action. While some community-based practitioners struggle to develop an approach that challenges notions of individualism and supports collective community action, a self-determined curriculum is sometimes reduced to individualized learning.

"On the one hand we are saying learner-centred is very important because learners who come to our programs have never been asked before what they want, and have never had anyone respect them when they say what they want. Learner-centred is an alternative that lets people see themselves in a new way. On the other hand, we want to build a

Learner-Centredness

consciousness of the kind of society that is good, that goes beyond what is good for me and how I am going to get there . . . one that contains a view of the world as a better place to live in, where everybody gets a fair share of the pie.

I think that somehow learner-centred means individualized curriculum. It is presented that way, at least in tutor training. The individual is seen as needing affirmation. But does this support collective social action or does it pull in the opposite direction because it stops people from seeing themselves as part of a group? It stops people from seeing that if they want to get anywhere, they have to get together. I find it tough to know where these two fit. And what makes it so tough is not just thinking about it as an idea, but actually doing it. For example, when you do learner-centred curriculum, you see how quickly learners can blossom before your eyes. And then when you do a group, there is such contention and it is such a long process before the group really develops.

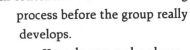

How do you make places where individuals can feel good about belonging and get affirmed, and yet, in the long run, build the connections that help people to define common interests? How do you do that? Because, in the short run, individualism wins hands down because society is built with those premises, and because we are not used to thinking of ourselves as people who work together."

This tension between the individual and the social (i.e. between the goal of fostering individual growth and learning, and the goal of supporting a collective or group learning process leading to social change) remains a continuing challenge. The struggle to develop and implement a self-determined curriculum that is also truly community oriented is the most significant and challenging aspect of the element of learner-centredness.

## LITERACY FROM A CRITICAL PERSPECTIVE

"What is literacy? Some learners come in hungry because they don't have enough food. Or, they are worried about their child they left alone so that they could come to the literacy centre to learn. What do we offer learners? Do we offer reading and writing, do we offer counselling, or do we offer to become friends with learners?"

When community-based literacy programs discuss what they do and with whom they work, they are struggling with a new definition of adult literacy. For those who believe that education is never neutral, the definition of literacy presumes, whether or not it is articulated, an analysis of and a vision for society. Precisely because of the marginal role literacy learners play within society, literacy education is very political. While all definitions of literacy tend to reflect the political perspective of the person or program that is doing the defining, community-based literacy programs are distinct within literacy education because they try very hard to articulate, not just reflect, their political perspective. More often than not, they acknowledge that their definition of literacy involves a social, economic, and political analysis of society. Inherent in this analysis is the indicator for the kind of educational program that will be designed.

The community-based literacy movement in Canada is indebted to Harold Alden for his analysis of literacy, delineating three political perspectives: **liberal**, **conservative**, and **critical**. Alden has used these terms to identify the political and economic assumptions that underlie the practice and theory of adult literacy and basic education in Canada.[8] To clarify how political perspectives relate to literacy programs, we have set up examples of how each perspective might be reflected in a literacy program model. While these examples are far too general to be authentic, they may help explain how one's political understanding of who literacy learners are can shape one's definition of literacy, and, in turn, influence the kind of programming that is designed.

From the liberal perspective, literacy education is perceived as neutral. Literacy learners are viewed as adult learners who, like millions of other adult Canadians, are taking advantage of opportunities for lifelong learning. The liberal understanding denies that there is a distinct profile of adult literacy learners that needs to be reflected in the curriculum and the methodology. The resulting program model is likely to be one in which the teaching methods reflect a knowledge of the principles of adult learning and the whole language approach. The curriculum is likely to include life skills and functional materials – all with the intention of better integrating adult literacy learners into society.

From the conservative perspective, adult literacy learners are perceived as being ashamed of their inability to read and write, living in fear of being found out. Illiteracy is described as a disease. It is understood that learners are seeking anonymity so that their friends and relatives will not discover that they have never learned to read. As a result, one-to-one volunteer programs are regarded as ideal since they respect the privacy of the learners. The belief central to the conservative perspective is that once adult students learn to read, they can go on to do anything. If they try hard enough they will "make it". The program model that grows out of the conservative perspective is one that is centred on skill-building . . . learning language by becoming aware of its structure and applying its rules. It is understood that learners will gain self-esteem by learning to read and write.

From the critical perspective, it is understood that adult literacy learners have the right to participate in a democratic society, and that it is the community's responsibility to ensure that all its members can be active citizens. The critical analysis suggests that literacy learners have little economic privilege as individuals and, as a group, are disempowered by their poverty. Illiteracy is seen as a reflection of a particular social, economic, and political system that does not equally benefit all groups within society. The process of becoming literate includes coming to understand oneself better within a social context and coming to understand the importance of actively participating in society. Literacy broadens the range of possibilities for developing one's identity. Language is created and acquired in order to better express this identity. Literacy learners shape, and are shaped by, language that reflects their cultural identity. A goal of the literacy program is to move this cultural expression into the public realm.

Community-based literacy programs aspire to the critical perspective. This can be seen in the vocabulary that the programs use to discuss the issue of literacy. For example, community-based literacy programs, to convey their understanding of literacy as a social and political issue, often deliberately use the term **literacy** as opposed to **illiteracy**, and the term **adult learner** or **adult student** as opposed to **illiterate adult**. Used from the critical perspective, the word literacy

conveys the notion of both process and content, more at the societal level than at the individual level. It is frequently understood to encompass the notions of advocacy and community education. In

contrast, the terms **illiteracy** and **illiterate adult** seem to convey an absence or a deficit within the individual and imply that illiteracy is primarily an individual, educational problem. This tends to reflect the liberal and conservative perspectives. The use of the word illiteracy gives a sense that illiteracy can be eradicated if individuals can manage to learn the skills of reading and writing, and that these skills will assist adults to take their rightful place in society. The word seems to speak of missed opportunities. It implies that, with increased literacy provision for adults, the literacy community will have righted any wrongs society may have committed, such as overcrowded classes, poor instruction, and (mis)labelling. What it does not convey is the notion that society, by its very structures, excludes some people and pushes them into lives of poverty. For community-based literacy programs, the term literacy has come to represent an understanding that literacy is also a social issue, and not solely an individual, educational problem. For many people involved in community-based programs, literacy education is a question of addressing social issues of inequity and injustice.

This effort to re-shape the terminology is an example of how community-based literacy programs are striving to promote a critical understanding of literacy. When community-based literacy programs define literacy education as something that involves more than reading and writing, they find that they are raising questions about their practice, their attitudes, and their values. For example, if literacy is defined simply as an educational issue, then it can be addressed within an educational framework; but if literacy is defined from the critical perspective as a larger social issue, then the educational framework is called into question and there is need to explore alternative approaches.

ELEMENTS OF COMMUNITY-BASED LITERACY

As community-based literacy programs seek to define what they mean by literacy and explore the implications for their practice, there are many instances where questions are unresolved and the resulting practice is a blend of liberal, conservative, and critical approaches. One such example is the relationship between literacy and employment. Community-based practitioners who work from a critical perspective know from their analysis of the relationship between unemployment and literacy that increased literacy skills may well be of nominal benefit in assisting many of the learners to find jobs. Practitioners who analyze the employment patterns and socio-economic situation of the group with which they work inevitably discover that unskilled, undereducated adults are over-represented in the low-paying service industries, where part-time, seasonal work is the norm and career opportunities are minimal. They know that if all Canadian adults were suddenly to become literate at a Grade 12 level, there would not be enough jobs for everyone.

At the same time, practitioners in community-based literacy programs subscribe to a definition of literacy that supports learners in pursuing their own interests. For example, when new learners enter community-based literacy programs asking how to complete job application forms, literacy practitioners are very helpful. They ensure that these forms become the basis of the literacy lessons. And yet, experienced practitioners have seen time and again how discouraged and frustrated learners become when they have learned to read and write better in order to fill out the job application forms, and yet still remain unemployed because jobs are scarce or non-existent. They have seen how learners blame themselves for not trying hard enough and for not succeeding. Nonetheless, when the next learner comes in asking for help in learning to fill out job application forms, literacy practitioners feel obliged to support this new learner in the same way.

In one sense, this is what community-based literacy means: allowing the needs of the learners to determine the content of the program and helping learners to achieve their goal to read and write. In another sense, community-based literacy programs feel they should encourage learners to explore the relationship between unemployment and education and to consider and take action around their own lives in relation to this economic and social reality. It appears that, within community-based literacy, there is as much an understanding of literacy as skills development as there is of literacy as empowerment. The understanding of literacy as skills development may also be supported by learners because, for some learners, literacy may mean:

> ". . . improving your finances. Because if you have your education, then the doors will open. You don't have to have a minimum-wage job. Literacy is fulfilment, a place in society, you know. That's how I look at it."

In practice, the process of defining literacy from a critical perspective turns out to be a very complex and difficult undertaking. When, for example, we ask practitioners whether they believe that programs ought to be shaped from a critical perspective and should therefore work towards empowerment and social change, the response tends to be affirmative. When we then ask how this is reflected in their methodology and curriculum, the response is often hesitant. Probing even further to see whether empowerment and social change are actually happening in the programs, we sometimes uncover frustration and exasperation as practitioners reveal that social change is more of an ideal than reality.

> **Researcher:** When students come in, do they talk about taking charge of their lives or changing the social structure, or both?

> **Practitioner:** They come in saying things fairly close to that. My student said, "I'd like to be able to go to the Eaton's Centre alone and if I could read, it would help."
>
> **Researcher:** Is that about changing the social structure?
>
> **Practitioner:** No, probably not . . . no. It doesn't change the social structure, that's true.

People taking charge of their own lives through literacy education might well be the beginning of a process of social change, but is this necessarily what learners request? The question then becomes whether the practitioner has a role to play in encouraging learners to consider literacy from a critical perspective, and how this critical perspective can be integrated into their learning program.

Given the desire of community-based literacy programs to explore literacy from a critical perspective, let us examine how this emerging definition is taking shape as it is being practised. In community-based literacy programs, literacy from a critical perspective means that programs assist learners to:

- improve their basic skills in reading, writing, numeracy, communication, life skills, abstract thinking, and general knowledge;
- increase their critical abilities;
- build self-confidence;
- increase their understanding of self;
- participate more fully in society;
- create language and culture;
- enhance the quality of their own lives;
- work towards empowerment and social change.

Each of these aspects contributes to the way community-based literacy programs define literacy. For some practitioners, these aspects are essential to literacy from a critical perspective. Others also find them essential but difficult to implement in practice.

## Improving Skills

Community-based literacy programs understand literacy to mean the acquisition of reading and writing skills by those adults who have difficulty managing the demands of our print-oriented society. In most community-based literacy programs, this includes learning how to:

- use the Roman script (such as left to right sequencing and alphabetical order);
- recognize the visual/sound correlation (phonics);
- recognize units of meaning (such as words, sentences);
- use the structure of the language (such as layout, structure of text);
- use the language (such as vocabulary, syntax, idiom);
- write for different purposes (such as grammar, spelling, formal, informal);
- write in cursive (such as forming letters, left to right).[9]

The emphasis on reading and writing instruction at a basic level distinguishes community-based literacy programs from other kinds of community educational programs, such as job training and second language training programs, where more advanced reading and writing skills are generally required or where the student is already literate in another language. Students of English as a Second Language (ESL), adults who are working on their high school credits through correspondence courses, and immigrants who have educational degrees from their home countries are not viewed as literacy learners by community-based literacy practitioners; nevertheless, it is not uncommon for ESL literacy learners and sometimes even literate ESL students to participate in community-based English literacy programs from time to time.

During our research process, community-based literacy practitioners and volunteers carefully explained that the purpose of their literacy centre is to be a learning centre, not a drop-in centre where people come in only to get out of the cold without particular learning goals in mind. Similarly, the mandate of their programs does not include providing daytime programming for adults who may have other needs but who are literate. For the most part, English-speaking students come to learn to read and write, and this is the essence of the program.

In addition to instruction in reading and writing, most community-based literacy programs also provide opportunities for learners to strengthen their skills in other areas, such as numeracy, communication, functional skills, life skills, abstract thinking, and general knowledge, although practitioners sometimes question whether literacy from a critical perspective includes life skills. Some community-based literacy participants consider life skills to be extremely class biased and shun the behavioural theories that underlie this kind of instruction. They question whether or not life skills are in the interests of learners.

### Increasing Critical Abilities

During our research discussions, community-based literacy practitioners and volunteers explained that an important dimension of literacy is:

". . . helping people to become critical thinkers";

". . . training people, not just to read specific texts, but to become problem-solvers";

"... problem-solving ... it becomes a tool which you could use to help you solve your problems."

Among those involved in community-based literacy, most agree that literacy provides an opportunity for learners to increase their critical abilities. Interpretations vary, however, as to what the term **critical abilities** actually means. Clearly, the word **critical** is not always used to refer to the critical perspective. We suggest here three different ways in which critical abilities might be understood and implemented in practice: **critical skills**, **critical thinking**, and **critical perspective**.

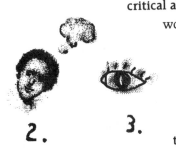

**1.**   **2.**   **3.**

### Critical Skills

In educational discourse, the term critical skills is generally used to refer to the skills of comprehension and analysis – skills that tend to be developed at a later stage in the process of learning to read and write. In essence, the development of critical skills includes being able to compare and contrast, to recognize patterns of thought, and to predict and deduce. This includes being able to answer open-ended questions such as "What do you think will happen next?", which require skills that are different from those used to answer close-ended questions such as "What did Bob say to Bill?" Teaching critical skills is part of teaching reading. In every elementary education program, instruction in critical skills is considered to be good practice and is included to help children learn to read critically. For example, one of the objectives of the Ontario Ministry of Education's policy guidelines for elementary education is to teach children how to comprehend what they read.[10] Every teacher of reading would be dissatisfied with a definition of reading that meant only decoding.

Community-based literacy practitioners, like other teachers of reading, acknowledge that critical skills are an integral part of learning to read and, therefore, include the development of these skills in their programs. Critical skills are almost always considered to be an integral part of reading theory. Reading, within everyone's understanding, includes the critical skills of comprehension and analysis.

### Critical Thinking

Whereas the term critical skills is concerned primarily with skill, there is another level worth exploring, which we have named critical thinking. Critical thinking, as we propose it, is the ability to see oneself in the role of reader, and to understand and analyze this in relation to the world in which we live. When readers develop critical thinking abilities, they are able to function in the role of reader as the creator of meaning. Critical thinking is at a deeper level than critical skills since it involves critiquing that which is in print. For example, learners are taught not to interpret the printed word as the given truth but to understand that each printed text has an author and publisher, both with their own reasons for producing the text. The learners come to think of themselves in relation to the text, as creators of meaning and as potential authors of their own text. An example of a literacy lesson in critical thinking is analyzing the images contained within advertising. In a printed advertisement, who writes the text? Why? What is the visual presentation? What is the content? What emotions are being conveyed? What ideas and messages are being conveyed? What personal/social interests are behind the text? What would a world without advertising be like?

Within the field of literacy, some literacy providers see critical thinking as more advanced and therefore inappropriate to the literacy setting, but this is not the case for community-based literacy programs. Most community-based programs tend to include the development of critical thinking in their daily practice, even with beginning readers. Community-based literacy programs profess that beginning readers are not beginning thinkers, and perceive this kind of lesson as integral to their program.

> "Every text is political and has a point of view. It comes from somewhere. Part of what literacy is, is to teach learners this."

### Critical Perspective

The term critical perspective, which we have drawn from the work of Harold Alden, is used here to describe the process whereby learners come to know themselves better in relation to their families, work, community, and society and come to see themselves as agents of change. The 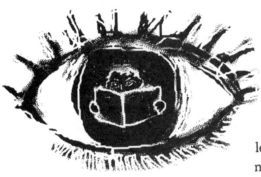 critical perspective is concerned with social justice and with creating an educational program that will question inequality and facilitate social change. An example of the influence of the critical perspective on a literacy lesson is examining the different numbers of hours men and women work in a day when women work a double shift at home and at work. This insight may encourage people to find alternate ways of organizing their lives and provide them with a deeper understanding of the inequality in gender relations, and how these relations are reproduced within the home and society. This is one way that students can begin to learn how to analyze their lives from a critical perspective. They look at their past and look to the future, developing an understanding of those forces (personal, economic, and social) that have formed their lives and shaped their choices. This type of social analysis allows learners to see themselves as active, not passive, agents in their own lives and within society.

Although discussions about how the term critical is understood and applied in practice still provoke disagreement in community-based literacy circles, most agree to some extent that the development of critical abilities is an important component of literacy education.

## Building Self-Confidence

> "Sometimes people don't understand. When I get confused, I feel ashamed. Especially if I can't deal with things that other people think I should be able to deal with."

Increased self-confidence for learners is considered integral to a literacy education; so much so, that it is often taken as a measure of success in community-based literacy programs. The more often learners attribute to their literacy education their recent gains in self-confidence or their ability to do things, the more successful the program considers itself.

In community-based literacy programs, even learners who choose not to measure their progress by taking tests or keeping detailed records of work completed still have a sense of their own progress. They communicate their sense of progress and accomplishment by describing how they feel about themselves as a result of being involved in the program. Many times, learners reflect that while they may or may not be able to read much better than before, they are able to do more because they feel more confident. Time and again, learners refer to confidence-building as an important aspect of their learning.

> "I don't see an improvement in my spelling. I do, however, see an improvement in my confidence. I go home feeling that I can take the world on."

### Self-Understanding

It is a goal of community-based literacy programs that students discover more about themselves – more about how they learn, what they want to do, and who they are as people. In community-based literacy programs, this may lead to a practice of encouraging discussion and self-reflection about people's lives and their personal circumstances. While practitioners limit the number of personal questions they ask learners, they encourage learners to share their life experiences with other learners. This respect for the integrity and privacy of people's lives contrasts with some of the personal probing that occurs in some other types of programming. In life skills programming, for example, the goals are not what the learners establish for themselves, but what society thinks is appropriate or best for the learners. This may lead to an over-emphasis on skills areas, such as grooming, nutrition, and housekeeping. In this approach, assessment and

evaluation is often done without the learner's explicit permission. Learners' progress may be assessed according to how much they have changed their appearance and behaviour, and this may be measured against the practitioners' interpretations of society's values.

Understanding oneself better, thereby opening up other possibilities of how to be in the world, involves thinking about oneself in relation to others: family, community, school, social organizations, work place, and so on. The hope for learners is that they will come to understand better the ways in which they have been formed by, and are forming, society; that they will understand how they have been shaped by the social structuring of class, race, and gender. While community-based literacy programs have no quarrel with the notion that most adults want to know more about themselves and improve themselves, they also propose that literacy education needs to recognize that sometimes it is society that needs to change.

## Participation

> "To participate is part of literacy learners taking more control over their lives and the forces that touch on their lives."

The concept of participation – using the language, rather than learning only the structure of the language – is central to the definition of literacy. Found materials, such as banking forms, housing and job application forms, and tenants' rights brochures are used by community-based literacy programs. The programs believe that people learn by doing – not by sitting in a literacy program and practising how to fill in forms in workbooks. Learners learn by going out into the community, going to the bank, or organizing day-care centres. Literacy as participation can be viewed on a continuum ranging from using found materials in the program to becoming active in the community.

Participation is also linked to the belief that a democratic country is only democratic if its citizens are well informed and active in the political arena. While many people would accept that Canadian democracy is not a participatory democracy and that literacy learners are among those who are least active, community-based literacy programs believe that part of the responsibility of a literacy program is to link literacy and participation, and to integrate learning with taking action on what has been learned.

> "One of the goals of the community-based literacy programs should be to have active students."

Literacy from a Critical Perspective

Increasingly, learners in community-based literacy programs are becoming skilled at speaking on their own behalf. Staff and volunteers work together with literacy learners to address issues that are on their minds – issues such as their children's success at school, child care, and the need for affordable housing or accessible transportation. Often, literacy learners meet with funders and eloquently defend the need for more literacy funding, informing funders that:

> "Literacy is knowing . . .
> where to get what you need
> where to change what you want changed
> how to say what ought to be said
> how to gather other people around you
> how to take charge when you want something different."[11]

### Creating Language and Culture

Another dimension of literacy involves the notion of creating language. Language is dynamic; we create language and language creates us. For example, we have many words to describe the world of work – a man in business can draw upon a multitude of words that describe and affirm his world. But a single woman on welfare has few words with which she can describe and affirm her world. Why is this the case? What positive words, and hence images, come to our mind when we are describing the life of a woman on welfare? Part of our inability to imagine this scenario comes from the lack of positive images and words in our language to describe poor people. This is because there is, in mainstream society, a lack of knowledge about poor people. Where, within the public discourse, are the images and language that describe and affirm poor people's reality?

Within community-based literacy programs is a recognition that the language of middle-class white Canadians is a language that excludes the experiences and the naming of the experiences of many different kinds of people – women, people with disabilities, Native peoples, people of colour, and poor people. It also excludes those people within our society who are not literate. In order to provide learners with an opportunity to use and create language that names their experiences, community-based literacy programs encourage literacy learners to express their thoughts and feelings through the telling of their life stories. In some cases, programs work together with students to publish these stories. In doing so, learners' experiences and reality are named. When books such as *My Name is Rose* from East End Literacy Press are published and distributed, they tell important stories, which need to be heard by others in society. *My Name Is Rose* documents the life experiences of a literacy learner who, as a young woman living in poverty, was forced to endure a life of violence until she managed to find a way out of her desperate situation. Through the publication of learners' writings such as this, the silencing of poor people is partially redressed.

By presenting a dimension of society that is often obscured, learners' stories encourage society to question dominant notions of what culture is or might be. Many learners are writing and publishing biographies, autobiographies, poetry, short stories, and other writings that are not only read by other learners but are entering the public realm. Some of these writings are seen as works of art in their own right and, as such, are contributing to society's definitions of art and culture.

### Enhancing Life

"As we come marching, marching, we bring the
    greater days.

Literacy from a Critical Perspective

The rising of the women means the rising of the
   race.
No more the drudge and idler – ten that toil where
   one reposes,
But a sharing of life's glories: Bread and roses! Bread
   and roses!"[12]

Just as the women's movement has articulated the desire for roses as
well as bread, the community-based literacy movement argues that a
literacy education needs to include opportunities for learners to
enhance the quality of their lives. This is the part of literacy that
might be seen to nurture the soul as well as the mind, beauty as well
as survival. Within community-based literacy programs, learning is
not only about skills or functional materials. While the programs
recognize that skills are important (for example, people need to be
able to decode a text), they want to give learners the opportunity to
appreciate the joys of language and culture.

"There is a rhetoric of literacy which asks: how do we
help these poor people, who can't read and write,
survive? How do we help them to get jobs, to get
through the social service bureaucracy, to get to the
bank, and then to manage their money? But there is
another understanding of literacy which has us ask:
how come, for people who are undereducated, we talk
about literacy as learning survival skills and coping
skills; and for those of us who were lucky enough to
get a good education, we talk about literacy as helping
us to enhance the quality of our lives, to appreciate
the world around us, and to have fun with language?

It's not fair that there are two classes of education.
I think that a lot of people who come to a literacy
program are people who feel ripped off by the education they got in the first place because they got

streamed into a basic education very early on. Literacy for them has always been how to find an apartment or brush their teeth or wash their hair, so that if they went for a job interview they would be presentable. Literacy was never how to appreciate the world of cultural discourse.

Why are there two standards? One for literacy learners who already feel ripped off because they were streamed into a vocational program. These adults don't deserve to be ripped off again by learning another set of functional skills.

I don't like the idea that literacy gets locked into . . . we teach people how to cope and survive. Because it's not fair that undereducated people only get to cope and survive and that other people in this world get to enjoy life. I think that there's a way we talk about literacy to the world, to the media, or to the tutors who go through the training. We need to think about that really carefully. Sometimes they come in with idealistic notions, like 'I want to teach somebody who's going to read great literature,' and it's not real because it's got nothing to do with where they're going to be starting with learners. On the other hand, some people come in and decide that they're going to organize somebody's life so they can cope better. There should not be such a wide gap there.

It's not just functional literacy . . . some things you learn just because they're beautiful."


## Empowerment

For community-based literacy programs, the notion of empowerment (the power to change one's own life) is closely intertwined with literacy. This concept can be traced to the influence of the Brazilian educator, Paulo Freire, who encouraged a radical pedagogy for the purpose of educating people to free themselves from oppression. This pedagogy calls learners to action through a process of liberatory education in which people learn to describe their exploitation and oppression as well as to reflect upon and analyze the forces that control their lives.[13] Theoretically, empowerment is integral to community-based literacy, yet programs struggle to find appropriate ways to use Freire's radical pedagogy with literacy learners in Canada. While fundamentally there is agreement that literacy learners can benefit by learning more about themselves in the context of their society, many difficulties remain in applying a Freirian methodology in a community-based literacy program. The reasons for this are complex and open to further study. To cite only a few, literacy learners in Canadian society:

- may have many of their basic survival needs met but are surrounded daily by affluence and consumerism;

- may have had many years of unsuccessful schooling, which have led them to believe that they are incapable of learning;

- are surrounded by the dominant conservative and liberal ideological discourses through diverse, multiple, and powerful media images.

Nonetheless, community-based literacy programs using a Freirian approach want to:

"... give people the tools to change their lives and empower them so they will make social change."

Arising from this goal are significant questions. What are the tools programs want to give to adult learners? How do staff and volunteers think learners' lives will change? How do learners think their lives will change? What does empowerment look like? What does social change look like? We further explore these questions in Chapter 3 where we look at the challenges that community-based programs face when they aspire to adopt empowerment as a goal.

## COMMUNITY-BUILDING

The third element of community-based literacy, which we identify as community-building, encompasses an exciting and creative process whereby people gather together in learning relationships that aspire to be equitable, just, and tolerant. This is the first step to building communities that are equitable, just, and tolerant.

"The word community comes from the word commune. This indicates sharing – a warm intimate form of communication. The word community should challenge us to find ways of sharing and listening. This is the highest form of a relationship. The word community is an ideal word for what we do."

In striving for "the highest form of relationship" among people, the term community-building is embraced by the community-based literacy movement. Community, as it is used by the three community-based programs, encompasses a number of meanings:

- geographical location, that is, the community as a particular neighbourhood;
- feelings that are shared between people and the atmosphere that is created;
- commonality of interests and concerns shared by people within the program, that is, an interest in learning or teaching reading and writing, or an interest in social change;
- resources that can be brought into the program from the community, such as people, money, services, and information.

These meanings of community are understood as part of the community development process – a process that involves collective action by community members to strengthen the community. Community development encourages commitment among people within literacy programs to build stronger literacy programs and among people within neighbourhoods to build stronger neighbourhoods. It also encourages a reciprocal relationship between literacy programs and neighbourhoods.

In community-based literacy, community-building means that programs:

- are located in the community at convenient locations, are open at convenient times, are responsive to community needs, and co-operate closely with other neighbourhood services;
- foster the development of common interests and goals;
- encourage literacy to be understood and practised as a social process;
- create a sense of belonging;
- draw upon members of the community to share responsibility for the education of other adults within the community;

- help learners to acquire an understanding of self in relation to society;
- work to build supportive communities.

### Community Location

"We're creating our own community in a sense. We're drawing in people from the area."

Among its many other roles, the commitment to a sense of community has been an organizing principle when community-based literacy programs set up their centres. As a result, centres are organized so as to permit learners to come to the programs anytime throughout the day. Located right in the learners' neighbourhoods, community-based literacy programs try to be easily accessible. It is considered important that programs be:

". . . within the geographic area";

". . . close by. You don't have to travel two hours to get there."

The focus on neighbourhoods helps programs to be flexible and responsive to the particular requirements of each community. Learners, staff, and tutors stress the importance of programs being:

". . . responsive to the community";

". . . oriented towards the specific needs and goals of the people";

". . . flexible – constantly changing. We change to meet the needs we hear people expressing. We don't

Community-Building

say 'these are our priorities' and then slot people into them. I think that's the difference between community-based literacy groups and a lot of social service organizations. There are very few restrictions for becoming a learner."

Neighbourhood resources are used, hence, members feel that they are part of something larger.

"We are connected with the community . . . the community-based literacy program has direct contact with other community-based services, so there is a deeper knowledge and understanding of what's going on."

And learners feel that other people will support them in achieving their goals.

"Everyone helps to identify what might be in the way of the learning process, such as a lack of babysitting or quiet time to learn. The program tries to address some of these barriers."

Community-based literacy programs are often seen by learners as a place where people can go for help, if they are in trouble and a place where others will:

". . . wrap their arms around people. If learners come in and say they have a problem with learning to read and write, the programs also know that this may mean that these learners also have a problem with another part of their life. And so you say, we're here to help with reading and writing, but we know where to go to deal with the other problem and the service is

close by. It won't take
long because it's only two
steps away or one block.
That's what it means to
be part of a community."

The community component is
especially important in low income
areas of the city. Extra resources to
cover the costs of transportation,
babysitting, and fees for service, such as
legal and income tax preparation, are not easily found. This physical
connection to the neighbourhood and to other community resources
is a valued component of community-based literacy programs.

### Fostering Common Interests

"We have a community of shared interests within the
program. People come to a community-based literacy
program because they share an interest in literacy."

This shared interest in literacy is the starting point; it is what brings
learners and volunteers into the program in the first place. Although
from different worlds with different aspirations, material realities,
and life experiences; learners, volunteers, and staff are brought
together because of their shared interest in literacy. People are
brought together and begin:

". . . working in common and having things in
common that we can all share."

Bringing people together from different parts of the community is a
priority for community-based literacy programs. The programs

place importance on bringing people together who would otherwise live in the same community but perhaps not know each other. These people get to know one another and find out what, other than literacy, they have in common with one another.

> "Community implies small. It is a group small enough to understand each other, to listen to each other, that has a lot in common. Now, we do not start off with a lot in common, but that is one of the reasons that we get together."

Ideally then, people begin to share aspirations for a better and stronger community – one where diverse interests are included and active participation representing these diverse interests is sought.

> "Community-building, for me, means bringing together people from different parts of society who wouldn't otherwise meet, so that they can share with each other what they know."

Community-building – sharing and building upon common interests – can be problematic. Members of community-based literacy programs struggle with whether or not differences between learners, learners and volunteers, and learners and staff can be bridged. For example, can economic differences, which are structural differences within society, be bridged in this way? The answer is definitely no. Economic differences remain in people's lives, whether or not they have found common interests within the literacy program or within the community. Members also struggle with the concern that economic differences are reflected and reproduced in literacy programs much as they are in society. Economically privileged staff and volunteers are the ones who teach; economically disadvantaged learners are the ones who learn. The different roles that are filled by staff, volunteers, and learners can lead to an unequal power balance that is weighted in favour of the staff and volunteers. Community-based programs strive for an atmosphere of equality, which assists members to become aware of, and struggle with, the unequal power balance inherent in the different roles that are assumed. Dialogue about how these roles lead to situations of privilege or disadvantage is what is unique and special about this aspect of community-building.

### A Social Process

Community-building encompasses an understanding of the social dimension of literacy. Community-based literacy programs believe that reading is not a solitary act. In the act of reading, there are always relationships between the writer and the reader, the reader and society, and the writer and society. Reading is the interplay of this relationship. It is neither solitary nor individual. It always involves more than one person and more than one world view. Reading, as such, is social. Recognizing this, community-based literacy programs try to approach learning to read in a social context. Learners are encouraged to see their problems with reading as part of a larger social problem that involves a larger social solution. Learners are encouraged to read and write together, within the program and within the community. Authorship is not anonymous. The relationship between reader and writer is continually brought to the forefront.

> "We help people to know that literacy is social inter-
> action."

In learning to read and write in a program where there is a social definition of the problem and a social understanding of the nature of reading, learners come to rely on one another for support and direction.

> "One of the roles of a community-based program is that it allows people to get to know each other and to learn from each other."

Learners are encouraged to work together, and in so doing, discover their abilities, rather than their disabilities; their strengths, rather than their weaknesses. Within the community-based programs, students learn how to learn together.

> "People are doing something together. They are not working in isolation."

The community approach to learning to read and write is sustained and nourished by the understanding that literacy is a socially constructed process.

## A Sense of Belonging

> "When an adult literacy learner walks in and tells another adult, 'I can't read and write,' it takes a tremendous amount of courage. It is important that when you walk into the literacy centre, the staff makes you feel at home. But it is not until you meet another student that you know that this is the right place and that these people are going to help you. At my literacy program, students took the time to help each other. They showed me around

the office and explained what was going on and
what kind of program they have. This was
important to me."

The organization of community-based literacy programs is based on
the belief that learners and others have a right to be there, that they
belong, and that other people are committed to them.

"Community helps you to not feel so alone or fright-
ened. It is important . . . If you don't have it, you
really suffer."

"Community means commitment."

These definitions of community-building, belonging, and commitment are ideals towards which community-based literacy programs
strive. They do this because it is important that learners do not feel
alone with their problem.

"Community makes you feel that you are not alone.
That other people have the same problems."

Through learning environments that draw on the strengths of a
diversity of people, learners become aware that they are increasingly
able to make a commitment to themselves and others.

"Before I came here, I kept putting it off. But once I
started to come here, I felt more like I could cope
with ordinary things in life. I felt that I could do
more things. Before I got here, I could hardly do
anything at all."

Tutors also become aware of their capacity to make a commitment.

Community-Building

> "There is a feeling of real warmth after you tutor. A real warmth because you have been sharing with one another. I think that connection is a really important part of community-based literacy."

Community-based literacy, in the process of community-building, helps in a small way to break down the isolation experienced by both learners and tutors.

> "People have a sense of belonging to something. Both tutors and learners have been isolated. This is a chance for people to come together, it is a part of learning."

While this sense of belonging and commitment is not likely to be unique to community-based literacy programs, those involved with the programs take great care to ensure its presence. On a day-to-day basis, people are made to feel welcome. They are greeted with respect, and thought is given to helping them feel comfortable.

### Sharing Responsibility

> "Members in the community share responsibility for the education of other adults within the same community."

Within community-based literacy programs, members of the community become informed about, and take responsibility for, the educational needs of other adults within their community. Ordinarily, the general public becomes involved in education by paying property taxes, voting for school board members, and keeping informed about the issues and concerns through the media and school-community meetings. The nature of community members' involvement in community-based literacy programs is very different. In a very intimate fashion, community members become directly involved in a variety of ways, such as volunteering their time to teach someone to read or becoming active on committees.

> "Community-based literacy programs create a co-operative feeling. Our people come up through the ranks. People who have control are people who are part of the program directly. They are in the program and also directing it. In some cases they're students. And I would say that is the difference between community-based programs and any other kind of program that I know."

In community-based literacy programs, community members become aware of the nature of the literacy problem. They become aware of the particular needs of learners and whether or not additional tutors, supplies, and study spaces are needed. They are intimately aware of the program's needs and take direct responsibility for helping to meet these needs.

Community members are aware of the scope of the literacy problem within their community. As active volunteers, they help to formulate policies that have an immediate impact on the program.

> "We learn about the process of literacy, the process of working in groups, and the process of changing the community."

Through this process of involvement, community members become politicized. Sharing responsibility for the education of other adult members in the community has the potential to make individual community members and the community as a whole more politically aware. Primarily, this is because community involvement leads to a

Community-Building

collective articulation of literacy as a social concern and a willingness to accept responsibility for addressing this issue with other members of the community.

> "Volunteers and learners, within community-based literacy programs, are people [together] making decisions . . . [they] are not a closed group of people who are making decisions about other people's lives."

### Part of Society

Members of community-based literacy programs know that they are:

> ". . . part of something bigger."

They are part of a community-building process, which includes:

> "people becoming participants in their society – people becoming participants in the community as well as more active in solving problems in their personal lives. Learners become participants in creating culture. They join in the discourse of literate people when they understand that they create culture."

This larger role is one that stresses the importance of learners understanding their role in the community. Acquiring an understanding of self in relation to society is a complex process.

> "In a recent issue of our student-produced newsletter, we talked about private and public life. The theme that everybody was working around was the idea of government, but they were really writing about their

own lives. So really what that issue is about is the relationship between an individual and the state. Learners came to realize: here I am, an individual and all the things that I want in my life, and here are these bureaucracies and they have powers that either help  me (for example, they help Martha to learn to read) or hinder me (for example, they hinder Joseph with immigration problems).

The discovery of this relationship builds all the way through. You start out thinking, 'What does this mean, public and private life?' and by the time you get to the end of the newsletter, it is all of a sudden really clear. You realize, 'I'm a member of my society' and you begin to see the relationship between your private life and your public life. You don't really kind of understand it all until you read through the entire newsletter and then all of a sudden it's, 'I get it – I'm not just by myself with all kinds of things just happening to me. There are some things I can control and some I can't. There are places where I can protest, where I can write letters and argue with the politicians and there are places where I feel helpless, and nothing I do helps. There are places where people make changes and there are places where no change happens.'

But you come away with the idea that you are located somewhere in society. I don't think this is empowerment. It's not like you feel more powerful

Community-Building

because you are in a literacy program. It's simply a discovery that this is who I am – in relationship to all these other structures around me. But the newsletter never directly comes out and says this. It never says, 'Your life is . . .' or 'The way that your life goes is controlled by this or that.' It's just people telling stories and by the time you get to the end you have discovered the relationship."

## Building Supportive Communities

In an urban setting such as Metro Toronto, where community life is tremendously fragmented and where many barriers to community-building exist, the building of supportive communities is difficult and arduous work. It is usually more challenging for literacy learners than it is for the general population, since most literacy learners have inadequate social support and must focus on more immediate issues. The poverty in their lives creates barriers to getting what they need, especially if what they need has to be purchased.

To highlight the importance of building a supportive community, we refer to the situation of a working mother who is poor. If her child becomes ill for several days, the mother's choices are to turn to her family, neighbours, or friends for help since the day-care centres are not equipped to take in her sick child. Although she would prefer to care for her sick child herself, she is compelled to find someone else who can do this. She must go to work. If not, she will lose pay and possibly even her job. The woman's family might be far away since her choice of where to live would have been made largely for economic reasons, not for reasons of convenience. She might live in a public-housing development that has been built and maintained in such a way that structural barriers are created between people, and support is hard to find. This woman, like many others, needs a supportive community.

Community-based literacy programs that operate in low-income and poor neighbourhoods recognize that building a supportive community is an essential part of their work. It encompasses a vision of nurturing neighbourhoods where people come together, develop respect for one another, and most importantly, begin to identify and provide for one another community support where it is needed.

The only limit to this vision is the reality that within poorer communities, community-building can be a long, slow process. The reality of poverty includes harsh living conditions that hurt the spirit. Inadequate housing, demanding work schedules, poor health, lack of food, lack of leisure time, physical disabilities, and inadequate transportation often cloud people's aspirations and their notions of what is possible. Some literacy learners may be confined by poverty to limited boundaries of thought and action. Part of the task of community-based literacy is to widen these boundaries and to assist literacy learners to articulate their aspirations for themselves and for their children, and to voice the demands that will strengthen, rather than limit, their aspirations. Community-based literacy programs strive to build supportive communities, working from the premise that community is essential for humanity.

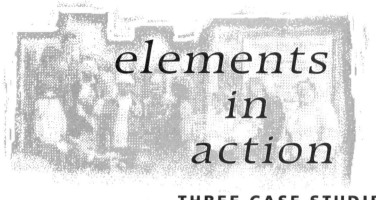

# *elements in action*

## THREE CASE STUDIES

This chapter profiles three community-based literacy programs in greater Metro Toronto, which were the case studies for our research: East End Literacy, Peel Literacy Guild, and Toronto Adult Literacy for Action Centre (ALFA). We look at the mandate, history, organizational structure, and funding, as well as learning and volunteering as they occur in these programs. (As part of the research process, each of the programs was asked to complete a fact sheet about itself. These fact sheets, prepared in 1988, are included in Appendix A.)

## MANDATE: STATING THE GOALS

Each of the programs studied defines itself as a community-based literacy program. What each program means by community-based literacy and the beliefs they hold in common are evident in their written mandates and goal statements.

East End Literacy sets forth the following definition:

"A community-based literacy project is one in which members of a community share responsibility for providing adult basic education. The acquisition of reading and writing skills is integrated with the development of confidence, competence, and understanding in all participants: learners and tutors, volunteers and staff. Community-based literacy programs thereby encourage community participation and development, involving adult literacy students in every form this takes."[14]

The notion of community is central to East End Literacy's statement. East End Literacy believes that members of the community share responsibility for the education of adults within the community, and that this educational process fosters community participation and community development. They place considerable emphasis within their community development process on the need for literacy students to be fully involved. In addition to the focus on community, East End Literacy's mandate presents a particular perspective on literacy – a perspective that defines literacy learning as an integration of reading and writing skills with the development of self-confidence through involvement in the community.

ALFA, a much younger program, looked to East End Literacy when developing its own mandate. Noticeable parallels between their respective mandate statements can be found, particularly in the emphasis placed on community responsibility, community participation, and community development. As well, in both mandates, the focus is learner-centred.

Peel Literacy Guild shares the focus on community participation with East End Literacy and ALFA, offering a learning process that is, in essence, a community learning process.

"The prime purpose of the Peel Literacy Guild is to assist adults in their quest to achieve reading, writing, and numeracy skills to enable them to enjoy full participation as citizens in their community."[15]

ArtWork

All of the programs share a common belief that literacy involves reading and writing, but also participation in, and development of, the community. This common belief in literacy, community, and the participation of learners has had, and continues to have, a significant impact on the development of all three programs and their self-definition as community-based literacy programs. A glance back over the history of each of the programs and a description of their activities provides an understanding of how community-based literacy has developed.

## PROGRAM HISTORY AND DESCRIPTION

### East End Literacy

East End Literacy, the oldest of the three programs, started with a definite community focus. The goal was to develop a community-based literacy program that trained local residents as volunteers to teach on a one-to-one basis and to undertake community education on the issue of literacy. The project began with a community worker and two community-work students. Following a survey of community agencies in the east end of Toronto, tutoring commenced in 1978. The community workers held information meetings, recruited members for a working group, and raised funds. A year later, East End Literacy hired a part-time staff person and began its first volunteer tutor-training session. As the program grew, community

involvement and participation were encouraged, initially in a small space provided by the city, later in a rent-free office in a community centre, and, since 1981, in its present location in a library house owned and operated by the Toronto Public Library.

In 1982, the program began to emphasize student writing and publishing as a learner-centred method for developing reading materials while helping learners to improve their skills. Gradually, more group classes were started, including a drop-in class. By 1984, East End Literacy was offering a range of programs and activities: one-to-one tutoring and small group classes; a student writing program; counselling and referral; a reading centre with a collection of resource materials; and community education and advocacy on literacy.

Today, East End Literacy continues to respond to the literacy needs of adults in a community where income levels range from welfare to middle class. Historically, the east end was the area of the city where much of the cheaper housing was built, especially for workers. In the area known as Cabbagetown, several blocks of old housing were torn down in the late 1940s in order to build Regent Park, then the largest public-housing development in Canada. Adjacent to this public housing, old Victorian houses have been renovated by middle-class families. East End Literacy adjoins these two communities. The east end encompasses many other residential areas including an industrial area that causes pollution and presents health risks to residents of the area. Not only is this community densely populated, but the population has grown and changed during the past several years. Regent Park, which was predominately an English-speaking, white, working-class population, has now expanded to encompass people of different races and ethnic origins.

ELEMENTS IN ACTION

East End Literacy's program centre is located in a Victorian house with other community services, and occupies two of the three rooms on the second floor. One room is used as the reading centre and houses the learning materials collection; the other is used primarily as an office. In the hallway outside these rooms, there is a small open area with comfortable chairs and a table where coffee and tea are available. East End Literacy has made good use of all available space, keeping the physical arrangements flexible so that the space can be used for activities ranging from one-to-one tutoring to small groups to general office work. The library house is a large, old inner-city house, which needs structural renovations and a coat of paint. Despite these inadequate physical surroundings and limited space, East End Literacy staff and volunteers have worked hard to create a warm, welcoming, informal atmosphere.

Although East End Literacy does not have a store-front window, it is relatively easy to locate. The library house is well known to many residents, and clearly visible from the street, with a large sign close to the sidewalk. However, East End Literacy is concerned that its second-floor location is inaccessible to people who are unable to climb stairs. For special occasions, when a large group is expected, they arrange to use a main-floor room in the library – a pleasant room, with a stone fireplace.

Recently, East End Literacy has been involved in negotiations with the public library concerning the future of the library house. Plans are now underway for the building to be renovated and East End Literacy will be given space in the building – space that will be larger, more functional, and wheelchair accessible.

## Peel Literacy Guild

Peel Literacy Guild was first established as a one-to-one
tutoring program, with the initial organizing work being
undertaken by a community-oriented librarian in collaboration with
two boards of education. By 1981, Peel Literacy Guild, through the
auspices of the Peel Board of Education and with the support of
numerous individuals and agencies in the community, had secured
sufficient funding to hire two co-ordinators and twelve full-time
tutors.

For the first three years, the co-ordinators and full-time tutors
met weekly at the Central Library. After the third year, board
meetings were held in offices at the Peel Board of Education, and
program staff was given a small office from which to work. All
tutoring took place in the community – in libraries, churches,
schools, restaurants, and people's homes. In 1985, Peel Literacy
Guild officially opened two offices
within the community.

The Peel Literacy Guild
responds to a geographical
community that is dramatically
different from the communities
of ALFA and East End Literacy in
Toronto. There are at least ten
distinct communities in the Peel
Region, a large area that encompasses two large cities, small
towns encircled by newly developed residential areas, and rural
areas with mixed farming. The region is characterized by highly
accelerated growth with a population that has more than doubled in
the last twenty years. Since 1981, more than 51 per cent of the
current population has moved into the region.

In an effort to respond to the different communities in the
region and the large distances between those communities, Peel

ArtWork

Literacy Guild decided to set up two separate offices. The Mississauga office, which is the location we visited as part of this study, is located above a retail store in a small shopping plaza. The plaza is at a major intersection where there are many other shopping malls. It is easily accessible by car, but can also be reached by bus. A

well-known retail outlet serves as a landmark, but because the Peel Literacy Guild does not have a sign outside the building, and street numbers rarely appear on the store-fronts, finding the office may be a problem for some.

Peel Literacy Guild has an area of open office space, with a few smaller offices, some cubicles for one-to-one tutoring, and an area for its resource collection. Although Peel Literacy Guild does not have enough space to meet all its needs, it does have slightly more space than either East End Literacy or ALFA, and it is in relatively good condition. It is well organized, and staff and volunteers ensure that the atmosphere is welcoming and friendly.

Peel Literacy Guild program participants are very pleased to have their own program centre and it is well used. Since they secured the space in 1985, program participants have noticed a definite change in the program. As one volunteer explained:

> "Before we had this location, we'd been in existence
> some five or six years, and everyone met in isolation.
> We'd hold an event, but it would take place on
> foreign ground, and often we weren't always
> successful as a result. Now that we have a home, you

see learners supporting one another, learners talking to the tutors, tutors meeting tutors. So when we have an event now, people already know one another. It's like an extended family.

Meeting in isolation can foster that sense of being embarrassed because you're a learner. In a group, nobody can tell who's a learner, and in a very short time people are feeling very comfortable with just coming . . . and they don't label themselves."

Peel Literacy Guild is an active and rapidly growing program. Currently, it is facing a major challenge as to how it might best meet the literacy needs of its large population, with its distinct communities spread over such a vast geographical area.

### Toronto Adult Literacy for Action Centre (ALFA)

ALFA is the newest of the three programs. Initial organizing work was started in 1984 by West End Literacy, a coalition of groups and individuals concerned with adult literacy and community development in the west end of Toronto. The ALFA program began in a church building just at the time that the church was being converted into the neighbourhood's first multi-service centre. The area is a mixed residential and industrial area with few social services. There are numerous factories, including a glue factory, an animal rendering plant, and a company that produces nuclear fuel pellets. Many residents are bothered by the noise and air pollution, and are concerned about health risks from potential spills of toxic industrial substances.

According to studies cited by West End Literacy prior to the formation of ALFA, this area was recognized as having a high rate of adult illiteracy, yet there were no adult basic education programs within the community. Through consultations among members of

the community, volunteers, and part-time staff associated with West End Literacy, a board of directors was recruited and a fundraising committee initiated. Gradually the program took shape, and in summer 1985, ALFA officially opened. Since then, ALFA has worked in collaboration with the neighbourhood community centre, participating on some of the centre's committees and on its board. The community in which ALFA is located is very diverse. Tutors are drawn primarily from the surrounding communities.

In many ways, ALFA has grown fairly quickly. The program continues to be active in the Davenport-Perth Neighbourhood Centre, and staff recently participated on a committee to design the proposed new facility. ALFA states that it has made many contributions to the design, emphasizing in particular the importance of easily visible and accessible literacy offices. ALFA houses a growing resource collection of learner and tutor materials, which is a deposit collection of the Toronto Public Library.

One unique feature of ALFA has been its involvement with the community newspaper, *Neighbours*. At the time of this study, ALFA, as part of its participation in the community, provided a full-time staff person to co-ordinate the writing and production of the newspaper. People from the community, from the Neighbourhood Centre, and from ALFA worked together to create each issue of the paper. Content focused on neighbourhood news and history as well as community issues, such as how to protest against industrial pollution. *Neighbours* has given ALFA students the opportunity to participate as both readers and writers in a more public print medium.

Program History and Description

"The newspaper is a place for writing for most people in ALFA and people in the community-at-large. It's also a place for developing skills, or using skills that you already have. It's . . . becoming a major tool for reading, discussion, topics, editing, and encouraging people to write other things."

During the period of our research, ALFA was encountering financial difficulties and organizational challenges that resulted in a reduction of staff. Also, the number of active volunteers and board members declined. ALFA is currently working to strengthen its volunteer and financial base, and continues to provide tutoring and small group learning, but on a smaller scale.

Although the space that ALFA occupies is neither large nor luxurious, the volunteers and staff have created a welcoming atmosphere. The building is a large, old, inner-city church in need of considerable repair, and ALFA's space reflects the general condition of the building. ALFA has the use of two rooms: an office and a second room where tables, chairs, and dividers are set up so that it can be used for tutoring and small group work. Tea and coffee are always available in this room which also houses ALFA's resource collection.

Unfortunately, ALFA is not easily visible from the street, nor is it accessible for the physically disabled. Since the space is located near the back of the building, it is necessary to follow a trail of signs through the building and climb more than one set of stairs. Although the current space is considerably less than ideal, ALFA is appreciative of the arrangement and hopes that renovations or a new facility will become a reality as the Neighbourhood Centre matures.

### The Learners

Learners in the three programs include English-speaking women and men, ranging in age from 16 to 70, some single and some with families. Although many were born in Canada, some are immigrants to the country. Few learners are fully employed. The majority find themselves in low-status, low-paying jobs and many others are unemployed.

While it is vitally important to understand who literacy learners are within society and within community-based literacy programs, very little illuminating data is available. In general, literacy learners' educational experiences have been short lived and interrupted by poverty, illness, family problems, or social problems. Many learners have fewer than eight years of formal schooling. An increasing number of Canadian learners under 40 years of age have obtained a grade nine education or more, often within a vocational high school, but still find themselves unable to read or write beyond the most rudimentary level.

We recognize that a socio-economic analysis is necessary in any effort to understand thoroughly who literacy learners are, but that is beyond the scope of this book. Nevertheless, we hold the belief – which we share with many participants from the three community-based literacy programs – that illiteracy is a reflection of poverty and that systemic oppression within our society politically, socially, and economically marginalizes adults who are illiterate.

Part of what we know about literacy learners comes from their stated reasons for participating in the programs. Some are parents who wish to become more actively involved in their children's education. Some who are employed would like to upgrade their skills in order to keep their jobs. Others who are unemployed or intermittently employed want to upgrade their skills in order to enter retraining programs or look for employment. Beginning from this understanding of literacy learners, the three community-based literacy programs provide learning environments that respond to the needs and interests of adult literacy learners. These programs have selected methods, materials, and evaluation practices that help learners shape and direct their own learning according to their own particular needs and situations.

## INTEGRATED METHODS AND MATERIALS

"Adults learn best when curriculum, teaching methods, and learning environments are geared to their experience, needs, and future goals."[16]

In community-based literacy programs that utilize the language experience story, methods and materials are interwoven. Learner-written stories, journal writing, found materials, and discussions form the basis for learning. The process of shaping methods and materials according to the interests of the learner begins when the learner first contacts the program. For the most part, learner participation is voluntary in all three programs. Learners are asked to call personally or drop in to set up an initial interview, even when someone from an agency has initially contacted the program. A staff person meets with each prospective learner to find out what he or she would like to accomplish, to explore areas of personal strength and interest, and to explain how the program functions. The learner discovers that there will not be a single, prescribed curriculum or set of materials. Instead, the learner has the opportunity to put together an individual learning plan, to identify themes of interest, and also to be involved in writing and developing learning materials. Learners also discover that there will be an opportunity to assess their progress in relation to the goals set out in their own learning plans.

ArtWork

### Learning Environment

During their early years, community-based literacy programs adopted a one-to-one tutoring model, which seemed at the time to be an ideal method for fostering a learner-centred approach. One-to-one tutoring is still practised, but in recent years community-based programs have been pursuing an alternative and complementary model: small groups. In addition to small group participation, learners are also encouraged to become actively involved as volunteers in the program. By participating as volunteers, learners are able to pursue their learning in a different form. All three approaches are described and discussed here.

### One-to-One Tutoring

According to the perception of one learner:

> "The big difference has to be the one-to-one. The schools don't give one-to-one. That is significant."

In the one-to-one tutoring model, a staff member matches one literacy learner with one volunteer tutor who has participated in tutor training sessions offered by the program. Generally, the learner/tutor pair meets once a week for approximately two hours. Whenever possible, learners and tutors meet at the program centre where staff

Integrated Methods and Materials

are available to answer questions. Otherwise, they meet together in other locations, such as the library, a church hall, someone's home, or some location convenient to the learner and tutor.

At any given time, program staff are co-ordinating and supporting a number of learner/tutor pairs. The number of tutoring pairs varies among programs and within programs from time to time. This variation is affected by the size of the staff, the availability of trained volunteers, and the way the program resources have been allocated. A significant factor, and a point of some discussion among community-based literacy programs, is the question of what is an ideal ratio of program staff to tutoring pairs. All three programs in this study recognize the breadth of programming that occurs in community-based literacy programs. It is considered extremely important to have an adequate number of staff members to maintain this breadth and also to provide the needed support and co-ordination for the tutoring pairs. Staff support for the learning process, which is only one aspect of community-based literacy programming, includes matching individual learners and tutors, recruiting and

training volunteers, monitoring the tutoring pairs, providing resource materials on an ongoing basis, and assisting in the evaluation process.

Some community-based programs have suggested that an ideal ratio is one staff member for twenty tutoring pairs. At the time of this study, East End Literacy and ALFA were operating close to this ratio. While it was evident that the staff was extremely busy in these programs, no particular concerns were expressed regarding the balance of staff to tutoring pairs. Since ALFA was experiencing budget cuts and a concomitant reduction in staff during the course of our study, its ratio of staff to tutoring pairs shifted, and it was

Darek Banasik/Canadian Living Magazine

ELEMENTS IN ACTION

facing a new challenge: how to provide adequate support to the tutoring pairs with a reduced staff complement. Peel Literacy Guild was in the range of approximately one staff member to forty tutoring pairs. During our research discussion, Peel Literacy Guild participants clearly expressed a need to assess this aspect of their work. They questioned how they could, with this ratio, increase their programming in community education and student publishing, while continuing to provide adequate support to the increasing numbers of tutoring pairs.

Another aspect of one-to-one tutoring is that, even though one-to-one encourages an individual approach, community-based literacy programs work from the premise that literacy is primarily a social process and not simply an individual process. While community-based literacy programs do take some steps to respect the wish for privacy expressed by some learners, it is the general practice of the programs to encourage learners to learn together in a community context. In practice, this means that learner/tutor pairs are encouraged to meet together in the literacy centre where there is an opportunity to meet not only staff, but also other learners and tutors. As well, learners and tutors are encouraged to participate in group activities, and many students attend group events as well as one-to-one tutoring.

One-to-one tutoring, as practised in community-based literacy programs, is an alternative to the classroom instruction that adults generally experience in many large educational institutions, such as community colleges and boards of education. While there are some community colleges and boards of education that do offer one-to-one, most tend to offer classroom instruction. For some adults the classroom is appropriate, but for those learners whose early experience with school was stressful and negative, the very thought of returning to a classroom in a formal educational institution is overwhelming. The community-based one-to-one tutoring model provides a friendly, non-intimidating alternative. Some adult learners, though they do not find the classroom environment intimidating, still seek out community-based programs because of the flexibility of hours, the individualized curriculum, and the concentrated attention that they receive in a one-to-one learning environment.

> "At the community college, you definitely have to know what you are doing . . . just like the workers, you have to have the tools. You would be amazed – like with music, you have to know the lines and spaces . . . They give you the package, so it's like a self-taught program. You have to read and do certain things on the computer . . . If you have a problem the teacher is there to help you, and students who are ahead of you, they help also. But you definitely need to know what you're about. You can't afford to be behind. Here [at the community-based program], it's at your pace. You can catch up because you're the only one who knows what you don't know . . . I think it's great. To me, it's like . . . the foundation part of it."

### Small Groups

While some students prefer one-to-one tutoring, others articulate a clear preference for learning in a small group environment that is more informal and learner-centred than learners might find with classroom instruction in a large institution. All three programs also offer some small group instruction.

> "With groups there is so much going on. When I am with other people, we write, we do things together, and so on. I think that helps me and I think that it is helpful to the others."

> "I think it's good for me as a student because I'm very shy. But the more I am out there, the better it is for

me. In groups we talk about all sorts of stuff. Somebody will say, there was a function earlier this month and I missed seeing you there. Things like that help. I think it helps."

ArtWork

"Students want to read and write, and communicate together, talk – things like that. But when you have a tutor, you're only talking to one person. When you have a bunch of people . . . maybe I'm tired of talking, then this guy might talk to me about his problems. And you sit back and listen. You learn a lot of things. What they've been going through and all that. I didn't have a good life myself but there's a lot of people who didn't have a good life . . . and they've been going through hell."

"I like a group because I have more fun. It seems the time goes so fast! We stay here until ten o'clock. But with a tutor you can't do that. Tutors get tired too, same as anybody else."

There are different kinds of small group learning experiences within all of the programs. For example, small group activities might include informal, weekly drop-ins or regularly scheduled small group sessions.

Drop-ins are generally scheduled at the same time each week and are open for any learner to attend. These sessions provide an opportunity for learners to meet with each other, as well as with volunteer

Integrated Methods and Materials

tutors and staff. The atmosphere is personal and friendly. Drop-ins are favoured by some learners because they provide a blend of group activity and one-to-one tutoring.

> "Everybody gets together, and if you're having difficulties, all I have to do is look at someone and they come over."

In some instances, learners come to the drop-in after they have already worked on a one-to-one basis with their tutor. In one of the programs, ALFA, the learner is given the option of participating in the drop-in or working one-to-one with a tutor. Since it takes some time to pair a new learner with a tutor, the learner is invited to participate in the drop-in until a tutor is available. Some learners who come to the drop-in first like it well enough that they decide they don't want to change to a one-to-one tutoring situation. As one learner explained:

> "We talked about a group at first because they didn't know and I didn't know. I didn't feel comfortable either in one-to-one or in a group. So I put it off. They called me. I said, 'I can't make it.' Finally, a good friend of mine suggested coming. I told her 'no' and she kept saying, 'You should go, you should go, you should go,' so I came. I came Saturday to the drop-in and it was really good."

For some learners, a combination of one-to-one tutoring and participation in the small group drop-ins is ideal.

> "I'll take them both [tutoring and the drop-in] at this point. I have high goals . . ."

In addition to the drop-ins, community-based literacy programs also provide other opportunities for learners to meet and learn together in small groups. The groups may be organized around particular activities or issues, such as the publication of learners' writings in newsletters or booklets, or a student action group. Within ALFA, student publishing primarily occurs in conjunction with the production of the community newspaper, *Neighbours,*and at the Peel Literacy Guild, student publishing is in the form of booklets such as *Write On* and *Write to Read.*

A staff member at East End Literacy describes the three different types of groups that were active in their program at the time of this study.

"The first one is the Women's Group, which is focusing on health issues – they're studying reproductive health now. The second group is the Writer's Voice group, which produces the publication called the *Writer's Voice,* but is also a group . . . There's more of a focus on group learning now than one-to-one, so group stories are being written. We invite resource people and have discussions and debates. The third group is the drop-in, which is very individual. It's a very small group which is responding to the needs of the people who are there."

ArtWork

At the time of this study, East End Literacy and ALFA began offering literacy classes in addition to one-to-one tutoring, drop-ins, and small groups that focus on particular themes or activities. These additional literacy classes were co-sponsored by a local community college with the assistance of government funding. At East End Literacy, the class initially included six or seven people who wanted more than once-a-week tutoring, but who also felt they

Integrated Methods and Materials

weren't yet ready to move into a formal, institutional upgrading class. The classes were designed to serve as a bridge, providing students with the opportunity to learn academic content that they would require to enter an upgrading class in a formal educational institution. These bridging classes mark a substantial change in small group work for the community-based literacy programs, and allow for a different kind of learning situation. For example, this was the first time that East End Literacy and ALFA had organized small groups to meet four days a week at a regularly scheduled time. Other small groups generally meet once a week. Also, learners who participate in the classes are provided with financial assistance for transportation and childcare. This was the first time that it was possible to secure this level of direct financial support for learners in the community-based programs.

### Students Learning as Volunteers

For many students, participation in the literacy program extends beyond their tutoring and small group studies. Often, students do volunteer work in the offices of the literacy programs, assisting with various tasks such as mailings, shelving materials in the resource collection, and organizing special events and social activities. Students are also invited to join committees and stand for election to the board of directors. One student member of the East End Literacy Board of Directors comments on his learning experience:

> "I decided to join the East End Literacy Board so that I could see what goes on behind the scenes, and learn how decisions are made. I also wanted to express a student's point of view at board meetings.
>
> Sometimes it's hard to understand what's going on because the meetings go so fast. I don't always get as much time as I need to report on what students are doing. Also, you have to remember that you have

to memorize a lot when you can't read and write well.

But being on the board is a good experience for me. I've learned a lot about how a meeting is run and how to organize things, and I've also learned how hard we students need to work if we want to achieve things for ourselves."

### Innovative Learning Materials

One of the most striking features of community-based literacy programs is the learning materials they use. Together, tutors and learners are encouraged to become familiar with a variety of materials, identifying those which best suit the students' interests and needs. These materials include commercially produced materials and found materials such as application forms and banking slips; however, there is a predisposition towards having learners write their own stories, using the language experience method and journal-writing. Learners are also encouraged to read each others' stories. This approach reflects the importance of beginning with what learners already know and are capable of doing, as well as respecting learners' values and world view.

The practice of using learner stories has led to the development of innovative learning materials for literacy. For example, East End Literacy initiated East End Literacy Press. This press specializes in producing student-written materials and has a national reputation for publishing easy-to-read adult books, of excellent quality. In 1985, East End Literacy Press launched the *New Start Reading Series*, which included six titles as of 1989. The active involvement of literacy learners in the development and production of the series is integral to its success. This has resulted in the introduction of creative methods for teaching literacy. For example, the publication, *My Name is Rose,* was developed from a series of photos dramatizing a learner's account of her life. Rose, assisted by the press co-ordinator, chose actors to portray her life in the photos, directed the scenes for the photographer, and was part of the team that selected the photos, designed the layout, and completed other tasks in the publishing process.

### Student Learning Plans

When a student first comes to the program, student and tutor meet together, sometimes with a staff member, to draw up a learning plan, which guides the curriculum over the initial six-month period. This plan is negotiated between the student and the tutor. It states the student's specific goals, the kind of approach and materials the tutor and student might use, and how they will evaluate their progress at the end of the six-month period. It then becomes the responsibility of the tutor and student, with assistance from the staff, to locate relevant and appropriate materials.

> "Here we're trying to offer a student-based, one-to-one approach. There's that personal tailoring, which is very subjective, as opposed to the objective curriculum . . ."

### Evaluation

"At East End Literacy, all of the program participants share responsibility for evaluating its successes and failures. Program evaluation is a continuous process, takes place in many different ways, and goes beyond measuring progress in reading and writing to include constructive planning for the community's program."[17]

The importance of evaluation for learners, tutors, staff, and board is stressed in community-based programs. Ongoing evaluation of the learners' progress is addressed weekly within the tutoring sessions. When evaluating the learners' progress, the program emphasizes learners' strengths. This is significantly different from what happens in many other programs where testing is commonly used for assessment and evaluation purposes. Whereas testing usually identifies what the learners don't know, the evaluation process in the three community-based literacy programs works to affirm learners' strengths and knowledge base. In addition to weekly discussions, the learners' progress is also measured on a semi-annual basis. When learners reach the six-month point in their learning plans, staff usually meet with the learners and tutors to assess joint accomplishments in relation to goals outlined in the learning plan and to establish new learning goals.

### Volunteer Development

**VOLUNTEERING**

All three community-based programs are incorporated as non-profit, voluntary organizations and registered as charitable organizations. Each of the three programs deliberately chose to adopt a voluntary organization model. Within this model, volunteers are involved in a variety of ways: tutoring; planning and decision-making at the board and committee levels; fundraising; assisting in the literacy centre; doing office work; helping to locate and develop materials; and planning special literacy events.

The voluntary organization model was chosen by community-based literacy programs because it provides an avenue for a

Volunteering

87

meaningful level of community participation in the program, and because it supports the notion of the community's responsibility for learning. The community-based, voluntary organization model, in contrast with other literacy provision models, such as boards of

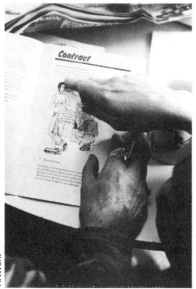

education and community colleges, allows the community to take direct responsibility for literacy in a way that reflects the membership of the community. The board of directors, as well as volunteer tutors, students, and staff are responsible for shaping the kind and quality of literacy education that will be available to adults in the community.

In the community-based literacy programs, volunteering involves community members – volunteers and learners – working together to build the community. Volunteers are invited to contribute to the program as a whole. For example, a volunteer tutor in a community-based program will be encouraged to become involved in the ongoing operation of the program and in making decisions that concern the program. In contrast, volunteer tutors in a board of education, community college, or large educational institutional program will be involved only with tutoring. When we think back to the stated mandates of the three programs, we note that each program views community participation and community development as important components of the literacy education process. Volunteer tutoring and other volunteer activities within community-based programs are regarded as work that will ultimately strengthen the community. Within this context, volunteer work has greater potential than in programs that operate with volunteers on a charitable model or with paid teachers.

The three programs see the voluntary organization structure as providing a route for community members to undertake political education and advocacy around literacy issues. East End Literacy,

Peel Literacy Guild, and ALFA have all been involved in such education and advocacy work. Within the organizations, this work is not limited to the board of directors and key volunteers. In community-based literacy programs, there is an avenue for all to be involved in collaborative advocacy work. For example, in all three programs, learners, tutors, volunteers, board members, and staff have been involved in attending public rallies, writing briefs to government, and organizing special events for International Literacy Day (September 8th) to draw public and political attention to literacy issues.

It is sometimes argued that substantial volunteer involvement within literacy education relieves the government of responsibility and contributes to continued inadequate funding for literacy. The three programs are conscious of this critique of the voluntary model. They recognize that programs that use volunteers may be less expensive to operate than programs that use only paid staff to teach learners, but they do not see volunteer programs as less effective. They have chosen the voluntary model, not because it is less expensive, but because it supports the process of community development. Community-based programs, given their commitment to this process and their recognition of the volunteer role in this, have consistently advocated for adequate public funding for literacy. In the case of their own programs, this has involved requests for sufficient staff to train and support volunteers to deliver high-quality programming.

### Tutor Training

The three programs provide initial tutor training for new volunteers and ongoing training for experienced volunteers. The goal of the initial training sessions is to introduce the volunteers to the organization and to establish the community context in which the tutoring will occur. The purpose of the ongoing training is to provide opportunities for volunteer tutors to meet with others in the programs, to sustain and develop their commitment, and to learn new methods and techniques for teaching reading and writing.

In the programs, the tutor-training sessions are continuously revised and updated. Increasingly, learners are participating in these training sessions, and all of the programs are experimenting with workshops that bring together learners and tutors.

> "We're trying something new . . . workshops that both students and tutors are welcome to attend. These are workshops that take up some interesting work that the student and tutor might be doing and that might involve somebody else from the community; for example, if somebody's trying to find out how to interpret the law, we make those connections available to them."

Tutor-training sessions may take different forms in each of the three programs, but the content tends to be similar. Sometimes, tutor training begins with a two- to three-hour introductory workshop that provides the volunteer with background information about the program and its philosophy, as well as an understanding of the adult literacy learner. This is followed by a series of in-service sessions once the tutor and learner are matched. At other times, tutor training is an eight-session course that provides the tutor with background information about the organization and the adult literacy learner, an overview of language acquisition theory and methodology, ways to find and develop appropriate learning materials, creative teaching techniques, and ways of carrying out learner-centred assessment.

All three community-based literacy programs have developed

tutor manuals to assist new tutors in becoming familiar with the goals of the programs. In addition, Peel Literacy Guild has prepared guidelines that reflect the values of community-based literacy programs. These guidelines govern the literacy instruction that is provided at the Peel Literacy Guild.

"Literacy provision in the Guild is based on the . . . understanding [that]:

- The program respects the adult status of the learner. Individuals are encouraged to take responsibility for their own learning. The tutor acts as a facilitator, rather than as a teacher. Acceptance of this concept demands an equality of relationship between learner and tutor based on mutual respect.
- Literacy instruction is learner-centred and responsive to the individual. Curriculum is devised on an individual basis, negotiated between learner and tutor, incorporating individual work opportunities for group theme work and confidence building activities. The methodology and learning materials take into account the culture, life experience, and knowledge of learners.
- The program is innovative in its approach to curriculum, methodology, and learning materials. The learning program takes into account adult needs, interests, motivation, and styles of learning. It is interested in helping adults learn how to learn, to use literacy to problem solve, and to engage in critical assessment. Although there are some commercially produced materials which are suitable, tutors, staff, and learners are encouraged to develop their own materials.
- It is a participatory program. Learners are recognized as adults who have the right to contribute to the development and governance of the literacy program.

Learners and tutors are encouraged to participate in program activities and to serve on committees and the Board of Directors. Learners are assisted in developing the skills required to contribute to the decision-making process.

♦ The program is committed to locating staff and tutors who have qualities which enable them to understand the learner's life-style, culture and experience."[18]

## ORGANIZATIONAL STRUCTURE

### Board of Directors

Each program is managed by a community board of directors, with volunteer board members elected from the community at the annual general meeting. Usually, the board includes tutors, committee members, non-tutoring volunteers, students, and people who live in the community. Each board also includes some appointed representatives from local school boards and other community institutions and organizations. While ALFA and East End Literacy each have only one appointed representative, appointed representatives of social service agencies and educational institutions comprise approximately half of the Peel Literacy Guild board.

At the time of our research, East End Literacy and Peel Literacy Guild had full board complements. ALFA was functioning with a partial board complement while taking steps to recruit and orient new board members from the community and to clarify their roles and responsibilities.

### Committees

Committees, an integral part of the voluntary-organization model, are vital to the day-to-day operations of each of the three programs. They not only sustain and support the program by undertaking activities such as program planning and fundraising, but also generate energy and creativity and bring forward community issues and concerns. Frequently, committees also serve as a place for orientation and training of volunteers. Committees usually consist of a small group of volunteers and one or two staff members.

Volunteer committee members are drawn from within the literacy program and from the community. Many are, or have been, board members or tutors in the program, others are interested residents of the community with skills and experience relevant to the work of the particular committee, and some are students. In this way, students become active volunteers in the program and work collaboratively with tutors, board members, and staff to help shape and support the program. In the community-based literacy program, student interests and concerns are sometimes presented and addressed by a committee of students. For example, at the time of writing, East End Literacy students were participating in the Students for Action committee – a committee concerned with issues of relevance to students.

Peel Literacy Guild has ten committees, while ALFA and East End Literacy each have six. All three programs have the following committees in common: personnel, fundraising, and publishing committees. When we compare ALFA and East End Literacy, we see that the list of committees is very similar. Both have program committees, but the major difference between the two programs is that East End Literacy has initiated an evaluation committee and an advocacy committee. Peel Literacy Guild has chosen to set up additional committees: an executive committee and property management, public relations, and nominating committees. One might speculate that these additional administrative committees have been necessary at Peel Literacy Guild due to the large geographical area served by the program, the greater institutional participation on the board, and the accompanying logistical challenges of having more than one program centre.

Organizational Structure

## Staff

At the time of this study, East End Literacy and Peel Literacy Guild had similar full-time staff complements: Peel Literacy Guild had four full-time and four part-time staff members as compared with East End Literacy's full-time staff of five. During the course of our study, ALFA's staffing situation was in a state of flux. When we began, there were four staff members at ALFA, three full-time and one part-time, but later in 1988, the staff complement was reduced, primarily due to lack of funds.

In each of the three programs, the staff works as a collective, with individual staff members taking on responsibility for particular areas of the work. This collective staff model tends to be a distinguishing feature of community-based literacy programs. Most other literacy practitioners who work within educational institutions, such as community colleges, boards of education, and large voluntary organizations, work in hierarchical structures. The use of the collective staff model in community-based programs fits philosophically with the learning environment – an atmosphere of learning among equals. Just as students and tutors learn and work together in the program, so too do staff members, who view themselves as part of a team of equals.

Among the three programs, there are some differences as to how the staff collective is perceived and how it actually functions. East End Literacy has a commitment on the part of the board and staff to the collective staff model. The staff divides responsibility for specific areas of program and these are noted in staff members' job descriptions. Steps are taken to ensure an equitable allocation of tasks, with everyone assuming a share of the day-to-day functions of the centre. There is no hierarchy and all members of the East End Literacy staff are paid according to the same pay schedule, which includes recognition for seniority of employment in the program. A similar model is followed at ALFA, although sometimes board members and staff have somewhat different expectations as to how the collective will function. According to the staff, this results in tensions from time to time. At Peel Literacy Guild, despite more formalized and distinct job functions, the staff also tends to operate as a collective. Staff members describe how this works.

"As far as the staff goes, we're a collective, pretty well. We all have our sphere of influence, there are grey areas where they overlap and then we consult with one another. But it's collective in the sense that we're all paid the same amount and are at the same level. And then we have three part-time co-ordinators, and two support staff. Still, in essence, no one lords it over anyone else. There is no hierarchy."

Peel Literacy Guild also has another distinct feature in relation to staffing. Whereas all the tutors at East End Literacy and ALFA are volunteers, Peel Literacy Guild pays an honorarium through the Peel Board of Education to approximately 70 percent of its tutors.

Staff in all three programs tend to be very committed, hard-working, caring individuals. Most do not have teaching certificates, although many have studied at the university level, some in education, particularly adult education, and others in related fields. Most bring to the program some previous volunteer or work experience with literacy. A member of Peel Literacy Guild describes their staff.

"Staff are experienced tutors. They were all tutors before . . . They have the practical experience. They're from this community with children in the schools. There's an element of being pioneers, at least in our organization. And we're so new that it's not like taking over the reins. You have to do a lot of the creating and developing of the roles. We still feel that we're breaking new ground."

Organizational Structure

Because community-based literacy programs believe they are breaking new ground, there are some new questions arising in relation to the staffing of programs, particularly in the area of educational requirements and accreditation. The position of literacy practitioner is increasingly being recognized in its own right but, as yet, there is no formal agreement as to what training or credentials should be required for the position. While community-based literacy programs have made it clear that they are looking for staff members with experience in the field of literacy or community development (either volunteer or paid work experience), there is more flexibility in their call for educational or professional requirements. Nonetheless, there appears to be some consensus evident among programs that they are seeking literacy workers who have some combination of experience in literacy, education, community development, publishing or journalism, administration, and voluntary organizations.

In the larger literacy arena, there are some tensions as to the educational qualifications expected of literacy practitioners. Whereas in most community college programs and increasingly in board of education programs, literacy teachers (including those who work on a part-time basis) must have completed formal studies in education and hold recognized teaching certificates, community-based literacy programs do not insist on this requirement. Rather, they are looking for practitioners who have proven experience at the community level. Because they are striving to offer an alternative to institutional literacy programs, community-based programs are reluctant to hire certified teachers unless they also have experience in, or clearly articulated support for, community learning. Since the learning environment and approaches in the community-based programs tend to be substantially different from those in the formal institutions, community-based literacy programs sometimes suggest that their staff need a different kind of training than that offered to prospective teachers, who will be working primarily in an institutional environment. Community-based literacy workers themselves are becoming increasingly aware of the need to explore the questions of training and accreditation.

Some community-based literacy programs recognize the value of having a range of experience and educational backgrounds represented in their staff. East End Literacy, for example, has followed this practice. At any given time, their staff has encompassed a variety of experiences: one staff member has experience in community journalism and has guided the development of their student writing and publishing program; another staff member has experience in the disabled community; another, experience in theatre arts. In general, while East End Literacy has followed the practice of having a staff complement with a spectrum of experience relevant to community and literacy work, the program has also been conscious of the need to have skills in education present in their staff collective and have, to date, always had at least one staff member who is a trained, certified teacher.

The staff members of community-based literacy programs are expected to take up new challenges as well as assume the responsibility for the day-to-day operations of the organization. Although the work is filled with rewards, it is hard work with long hours, many responsibilities, and poor remuneration. The intangible rewards offered to the staff, such as a creative working environment and personal fulfilment, have influenced staff  members in the two older programs to stay involved for three to five years. This continuity of staff, with some new staff coming in at intervals, has proven to be a good balance for East End Literacy and Peel Literacy Guild over their first ten years of programming.

## ORGANIZATIONAL DEVELOPMENT

A healthy organizational development plan and program is central to the successful operation of any voluntary organization. All three of the programs understand and acknowledge the importance of taking regular "temperature checks" to ensure the long-term health of their program, including organizational reviews, planning meetings, and ongoing evaluation. Despite the considerable time and resources that are required to undertake organizational reviews, each program has committed itself to this kind of self-evaluation.

The diverse areas of evaluation and research undertaken by community-based literacy programs illustrate the ongoing interest in evaluation. For example, during the period of this study, Peel Literacy Guild was in the process of an organizational assessment to assist them in exploring questions, such as how to provide quality literacy programming to a large geographic area given limited resources, and how to retain a community atmosphere and environment within the program. ALFA, at the end of its first year of programming, asked its program committee to conduct an evaluation. Through this process, learners' needs in the area of transportation and childcare were clearly documented. It was also established that ongoing organizational development work was needed. To this end a new board manual was prepared and orientation sessions for new board members were conducted. Over the last ten years, East End Literacy has conducted several evaluations, including a participatory program evaluation with an outside researcher, a survey prepared in collaboration with learners to determine their priorities, and an evaluation of their new bridging classes.

All three programs began with small seed grants, and as the programs have gradually matured, their budgets have increased considerably. In contrast with other literacy programs, particularly those operated by educational institutions, the budgets of community-based literacy programs are very small in proportion to the nature and quality of literacy education that is delivered. Although each of the three programs operates with a relatively small annual budget, a major ongoing challenge is to secure adequate funding so that the programs can meet their annual objectives. Responsibility for securing adequate funding rests with the board of directors, while much of the day-to-day support work for fundraising is done by program staff in collaboration with volunteers from the fundraising committee.

Despite the fact that there have been many disappointments, the three programs have been moderately successful in their fundraising endeavours. As is the case for many small voluntary organizations, fundraising has required, and continues to require, a great deal of staff and volunteer time, energy, expertise, and commitment. In each program, the fundraising committee meets regularly with staff to devise, monitor, and implement the annual fundraising program. Given that it is often difficult to predict whether and when grants will actually be received, the board and staff are constantly monitoring cash flow and income projections in an effort to ensure the uninterrupted operation of the program. Since most of the funding sources do not guarantee an ongoing commitment, there is always the possibility that the program might not receive sufficient funds to continue operating in subsequent years.

Historically, it seems that each program has managed to secure multiple-year donations at important points in its history. In the case of East End Literacy and ALFA, each program received a three-year foundation grant at a formative time in their early years. This allowed them to do some of the developmental work necessary to shape and strengthen their programs. East End Literacy and Peel Literacy Guild also received from the federal government job development grants (from different departments at different times), which allowed them to increase staff. With the increased staff, they were able to not only improve the quality and scope of their respective programs, but also strengthen their fundraising capabilities. ALFA, as the youngest program, continues to struggle forward with a less than secure funding base.

For all three programs, fundraising creates an ongoing tension. While programs know that they are providing valid and meaningful literacy education for adults for whom no other appropriate programs exist, they are often challenged by funders, potential funders, and others to assess their program in terms of cost-effectiveness. In general, programs assert that they do provide a cost-effective alternative (i.e., they provide relatively inexpensive learning opportunities for adults), but they also know that their programs are strained by the required volunteer and staff fund-raising efforts to secure core funding. There is a concern that this

fundraising work, which is not required of literacy workers in programs located within the public educational system, is drawing volunteer and staff resources away from the literacy education and community development efforts of the program.

During the past few years, some core funding for community literacy programs has been made available by the Ontario government. At the time of writing, all three programs are drawing a portion of their budgets from this source. The programs are pleased to have this provincial government support and are continuing to work hard to secure multi-based funding arrangements to cover their operations. Specifically, they solicit funds from a variety of sources such as local, provincial, and federal governments, and boards of education. In order to maintain multi-based funding that will enhance their autonomy, programs are also continuing to solicit funds and support from foundations, libraries, churches, businesses and corporations, labour unions, social service agencies, other community groups, and individual donors. The Peel Literacy Guild also holds special fundraising events such as bingo games. While the community-based programs are working toward a sound funding base, the amount available to them is minuscule in comparison with the amounts available to other adult education centres of learning, such as universities and community colleges.

# *elements in interaction*

## ISSUES IN COMMUNITY-BASED LITERACY PROGRAMS

Each of the three community-based literacy programs participating in this research study were asked to identify a key issue that either creates tension within the program or poses a difficult dilemma for it. The programs expressed hope that their honesty in exploring these tensions and dilemmas would serve to better illuminate not only some of the difficulties that occur when operating community-based literacy programs, where expectations are wonderfully high and resources are limited, but also some of their achievements.

These issues are presented as they were articulated by the programs at the time of this research project. Each group identified the issue that most concerned its program. Participants were then asked to consider the issue in relation to three questions:

- ◆ How do you know this is an issue for your program?
- ◆ How does your program respond to this issue?
- ◆ Describe where, in your program, you feel that the issue is close to being resolved.

The discussions that follow resemble those which took place when the questions were posed to the three programs, and each is written in the voice of the program raising the issue.

## ISSUE: MEETING COMPETING NEEDS

"Within our program, it appears as though there are competing needs of learners, staff, volunteers, board members, and funders. Each group within the program has its own needs and yet there are limited resources, making it impossible to meet everyone's needs. Given that we are committed to a community-based model, one which prides itself on meeting the needs of the whole community, how do we go about meeting all these needs?"

**How do you know this is an issue for your program?**

"I keep thinking of that commercial for fitted sheets. You run here to cover this spot and that spot comes up, then you run to that side and you grab that part, and the other side comes up – so you always feel that you're being forced to choose what's more important to attend to right now, and it's a false choice. Not because you necessarily feel that it's more important to have a resource collection than it is to do more research on how to get a tax exemption and save lots of money as a way of fundraising, or to investigate how to get placement students, which would cut down on the work. It's not really that one has sat down and thought, 'Is this really more important to do than that?' Sometimes you suddenly

realize I'm doing this
because it's here and it's
on the plate."

From the commitment to
learner-centredness in community-
based literacy programs, it is
understood that the needs of
learners – helping them articulate
for themselves what it is that they
want to accomplish within the program – take precedence. This
process, which encourages a kind of self-discovery, is undertaken
with each learner and to a lesser extent with each tutor, volunteer,
and board member. Staff, in particular, experience the tremendous
effort required to sustain this one-to-one attention for everyone.

> "We have to stretch ourselves ridiculously, in order to
> uphold our commitment. Not because there are too
> many learners, but because there are so many other
> things to take care of besides learners. We want to
> spend time with them, to be able to drop everything
> when they come in the door. We want to be able to
> make them feel welcome and heard. But there are
> many other demands on our time."

Even though working with volunteers is an integral part of
community-building, there are moments when staff members feel
that by meeting the needs of volunteers, they are diverting resources
that are meant for learners.

> "Sometimes our tutors come here with different
> interests from what we claim to be providing in
> terms of community-building. Sometimes tutors
> have extra time that they want to spend in a useful

Issue: Meeting Competing Needs

way with 'poor unfortunate illiterates,' or they come in hoping to teach skills in reading and writing, using a phonetic approach and the Dolch reading list of words. The different interests and different perspectives create a situation where meeting everyone's needs is difficult. I think the way these interests play themselves out every day is reflected in the tension we feel. We wonder what to do first: do we respond to a board member who wants us to spend our time checking out accrual versus cash-based for our audit, or do we spend that time thinking about the next event we're planning, trying to involve as many people as we can?"

Active volunteers and learners, as well as staff, sometimes wonder about how to set priorities in a community environment where everyone's interests and perspectives are given equal weight. In a given week, staff may spend more time with new volunteers and funders than with literacy learners, which creates a feeling that the priorities have not been respected.

"We often feel that we are not a literacy program, but rather a program for educated people, because we spend more time talking to the volunteers, tutors, and board members than to learners. We addressed that head on and made a really concerted effort to turn that around. We had somebody on our board, who had no experience with literacy, who continually raised questions with which we, because he was well respected on our board, had to deal.

That is partly why the staff felt we were spending more time with educated people than with learners. And because literacy is now in the 'news,' we are always getting calls from people, 'I want to volunteer. What can I do?' You feel that it's really important to make sure that they've got a good understanding of the issue, but then you spend your time with those people instead of doing things with learners."

Volunteer tutors also express a fear that, within their tutoring sessions, they are not giving learners as much as they ought to be giving them.

"As a tutor, I've always felt my learners wanted more. They needed much more than I could give them. They work so hard. I've always felt ashamed that I could give them so little time."

In part, the expression of competing needs as the most pressing issue is a result of the high expectations that people within community-based literacy programs place upon themselves.

"The kind of person who is attracted to working or volunteering at a community-based literacy program is the kind of person who is really concerned about doing a high quality job."

"We want to have as much contact with students as possible. And yet the reality is, sometimes, with all that goes on in the program, we don't have enough time to do that well."

But mostly the dilemma of competing needs is a direct result of underfunding. There are all kinds of hidden maintenance tasks in community-based literacy, such as administrative work, fundraising,

Issue: Meeting Competing Needs

clerical work, and housekeeping. This work is not funded. In addition, there are other kinds of hidden innovative work, such as organizational development, leadership training, information and referral, and community development, none of which is funded.

"For us, community-based literacy is part of our vision for a better world – a world of justice, equality, and citizen participation. But the vision is not fundable; the products are. In order to survive, community-based programs juggle both – but usually by staff and volunteers overworking."

"One of the concerns is that there are not enough funds, and that has a real ripple effect. Funding for community-based literacy programs is very tenuous. The expectations that are placed on staff by the program, the community, and the funders are enormous."

"Fundraising takes staff away from the program. When staff are out raising money to keep this place going, they're taking time that they could be giving to us learners and instead they're out trying to get more money to keep this place running."

This lack of funding limits the potential of community-based literacy programs and has other consequences as well. It can mean that programs feel compelled to accept funds from government departments whose intentions and beliefs about literacy are different from their own.

"We receive money to conduct a group that meets two nights a week. Lots of students in our program said they wanted more tutoring time than just once a week. But there are restrictions on how we operate the program, such as if learners don't attend more than three times in a row, then they're automatically out of the program. We are to tell them that they can never enroll in this kind of upgrading program again. If we are learner-centred, how do we justify this? Obviously the needs of the learners aren't being met by rules that say if they miss three times in a row, they can't ever come back."

Program participants are afraid that, in their efforts to keep their programs open and functioning, they are being pulled away from the community-based literacy model.

"We became involved in literacy because we wanted to work with literacy learners. But we have ended up becoming fundraisers and administrators."

Ultimately, this means that community-based programming is threatened.

"In truth, we are afraid that we will become exactly what the funders want us to become rather than becoming what we want to be."

**How does your program respond to this issue?**

The program utilizes a wide range of strategies for maximizing its resources including:

Team work:

"Surprisingly enough, in the middle of it all there's a real coming together, and a lot of creativity that comes out of moving at high speed. Team work happens in ways that you couldn't plan for it to happen. People come together, putting in all their gifts, and make something much more imaginative happen."

Better board recruitment:

"We're trying to recruit board members who understand something about literacy."

Self-evaluation:

"I've seen this program grow in the last two years, starting from an empty, dirty little room to a very good program. I think that's mainly due to the commitment and vision of staff and the real seriousness with which the planning is done . . . the checking and the continual self-evaluation, the comparing of programs, learning from others, and the self-criticism. Staff are never satisfied with what's happening and always want to make it better."

Increased advocacy:

"I think we may have to cut back, despite the need we see. What we really need are well-funded, well-organized, well-developed umbrella groups and advocacy groups. We need to know that these groups are dealing with the broader issues, and are having input into, and advocating for, appropriate policy on literacy."

**Describe where, in your program, you feel that the issue of competing needs is close to being resolved.**

ELEMENTS IN INTERACTION

Increased programming for and with learners emerges as the priority.

> "Once, at a social event with learners, staff, board, and volunteers . . . there was a real feeling that we had achieved something! There was a lot of closeness, lots of ideas, and people wanted to stay. And there was a strong feeling of community. We felt proud of what we'd achieved and that we were going on and were going to do better."

> "Whenever learners are part of the process, it is really good and everything seems worthwhile."

> "Once, I was staying late and there were three pairs meeting for tutoring sessions, a committee meeting was going on, a small group meeting, and the newspaper was being produced. It was just hopping. I thought, 'Oh, we really do have a good program here. Look at all these people.' Everyone was acknowledging each other, waving and talking. I had the feeling that the program was really functioning – that it was alive and well and very exciting."

> "The groups really work. There is a Saturday afternoon drop-in group. There is such energy there. There is a high level of commitment, trust, and respect."

> "As a result of our discussions about learner-centred, we have already begun to see changes. We involve the students a lot more. More students come by the centre, and more tutors and volunteers have become involved with the program. At the last workshop we held, there were thirty people. The majority of the

Issue: Meeting Competing Needs

participants were learners. We used to have tutor workshops but now we have joint workshops, with learners and tutors. Everyone loved talking to each other, no one left on the dot of five."

"We have made real progress. In the groups we run, there is always high attendance. More and more

learners are writing for the community newspaper. Our board has been changing and is coming closer to our ideal, and learners are becoming more involved in our tutor training sessions. There are many areas that we want to continue to work on, but I think we have progressed."

Through the experience of trying to meet competing needs, choices have been made, and these choices have favoured learner involvement. During social events, on busy evenings, and during drop-ins, the active involvement of learners illustrates that programming works best when it is centred on learners' needs. By comparing this programming with earlier periods, participants have a strong sense of their progress: they are consciously choosing, not just accepting, which needs will be met.

## ISSUE: COPING WITH GROWTH

"Within our program, we have to face the reality that there are many more learners in the community who need our program than we have resources with which to work. How do we continue to deliver a high-quality program to an ever-increasing number of learners? How can we turn literacy learners away? What gets sacrificed? How do we continue to grow?"

## How do you know this is an issue for your program?

"I wonder if in a perfect world one couldn't have an adult literacy centre of the same calibre as the municipal civic centre or the board of education building. City and board of education officials get incredible buildings and they, after all, can read and write.

Aren't we doing things the wrong way around? Couldn't the people who read and write make do, so that people who can't read and write could have an adult literacy centre? The civic centre and the board of education building is at such an incredibly higher level than anything our literacy learners have or will ever have. If we had such a facility we could have a day-care centre, day-time classes, and the learners would get subsidized while they were learning to read. We have the people and the commitment – it's just that society does things the wrong way around."

The anguish expressed in this plea for society to reflect on its priorities is relevant to the issue of coping with growth. Part of the struggle with the issue of growth is that resources for literacy within society and within community-based literacy programs are limited. The question for this program is how do they, with integrity, assist learners in identifying their educational needs within a climate of limited resources? And what do they do about the increasing number of learners who want to take part in their program, and the limited spaces for these learners? How can they continue to grow as

a program and also continue to provide a high-quality educational program for each and every learner?

"We have been struggling with this at the staff level and at the board level. We are a growing community and new people are always contacting us. Partly it is because we have been in the community a fair length of time. We have built up a good reputation and the community knows about us. We're getting more referrals and more word-of-mouth contacts. Learners come in and say, 'My friend Joe came here, and I want to come here too.' And we have a lot of tutors as a result of the increase in media coverage. We've had a 30 percent increase and it has stretched us like a rubber band. We don't even know everyone in the program by name. We decided to hold off on another tutor training. We don't have any physical space left; we cannot take anybody else. The region we work in covers such great distances. There was interest in starting a program in an area that is an hour's drive from this community and we are not sure how to handle that."

One inevitable consequence of expanding a program that already has limited resources is that the program takes on more learners than it really is able to handle.

"There are a large number of referrals to our program and we don't always have enough tutors

for the learners. The waiting list keeps growing
larger. We have too many learner/tutor pairs for
one co-ordinator to manage. We now have a ratio
of forty learner/tutor pairs to one staff person."

"We had another tutor training recently. The dust is
still hanging in the air. It hasn't settled at all. There's
no way we can do the kind of job we want to do. We
won't have enough time to get the matches going
before another training is necessary."

It is not appropriate to take on too many learners, nor to turn new
learners away. First, in order to identify and understand the scope
and nature of the literacy problem, literacy programs must be
known in the community as places where all literacy learners will be
welcomed. Second, it is woefully inappropriate to turn away literacy
learners who may have spent several years gaining the courage to
approach the program.

"Where do you draw the line and say 'no more'? It is
difficult for staff because we don't like to say no to
people."

One solution, again an inappropriate one, is to cutback on the
breadth of the programming.

"You begin to think that important components of the
program, such as professional development, tutor
support, and learner/tutor events are frills. And they
are not."

"We would like to form groups around social issues
but our staff is so busy with their first commitment –
to teach literacy learners to read and write. How will

we find the time to develop our practice? We could have fifteen offices in this region alone and it would not meet the need adequately. If we are a quality program then we should be doing a broader range of things. The program should offer more than simply tutoring. There should be many different kinds of groups."

"We have all been tutors and we know what that is like. We know the kind of support we wanted as tutors. We really go out of our way to provide support and it is draining us."

The issue of coping with growth is an immediate and pressing issue. It is also an issue for the future.

"How do we keep the program running and plan for the future, for this high-quality program that we are talking about, when we don't have any security? Some people think that because we are community-based it means that we don't need much govern- ment money. They think the community will be responsible. It doesn't work that way."

"We wanted to start a learners' drop-in group, as a way of helping people who are on the waiting list. But our centre is too small. We have to come up with some answers. How are we going to expand? We know we should expand but how are we going to do that?"

**How does your program respond to this issue?**

The program responds in a variety of ways, some of which are unsatisfactory, including:

Working overtime:

> "We work a lot of overtime to address the growing need."

Limiting the scope:

> "Some members of our staff don't participate in the networking groups nor do they have as much contact as they would like with the other literacy programs in the city."

> "We don't explore, as we might, other ways of defining literacy. We don't look at literacy broadly enough – towards a social definition if you will."

> "We don't advertise to learners, and we don't find those people who haven't found us."

Using our creativity:

> "There is a tremendous amount of energy, enthusiasm, experimentation, commitment, and creativity within our program."

"Re-visioning" the mandate:

> "We are moving towards the recognition that our program is a community program, which means that

the community has the right to participate. That means everybody. We don't want to 'use' tutors, we want tutors who come and participate. We don't want to 'teach' learners, we want learners who have a lot to contribute and who participate as equal members."

**Describe where, in your program, you feel that the issue of coping with growth is close to being resolved.**

For this program, learners' stories of achievement are the measure of success.

"I remember this student who wanted to work as a caretaker. That was his dream. But the [company] made him read in front of eight people. They didn't hire him because he couldn't read. This got me really upset. His tutor and I typed up a letter of complaint and we sent it off. We said that he is trying to learn to read and write and that he is dependable. A week later he got the job!"

"I taught a woman who was labelled mentally retarded. She is forty-three years old. She spent thirty years in an institution, when it was still called a residence for idiots. We worked together for quite some time. Now she lives independently in an apartment. One evening I went over to her place to help her sew some curtains. We talked about this and that. I was shocked to discover how much she had saved on her minuscule salary at the sheltered workshop. While I was there, I observed her writing out a cheque to the cable company. I sat back and I said to her, 'You know . . . you have really made it.'"

ELEMENTS IN INTERACTION

"There are moments – not necessarily long stretches,
but moments. I think Wordsworth called them, 'spots
of time.' Sometimes it's a smile or a radiance.
Sometimes it's a feeling. You know that person's life
has changed forever. Sometimes we talk about testing
or plotting learners' progress on charts, but in fact,
some of the best things in our lives are the things
that cannot be measured. That is because they are
intrinsic, they are experiences within. You can't
measure the happiness a learner has when she finally
knows how to write a word when she couldn't before.
The thrill of that for her cannot possibly be
measured, expressed, or articulated. We can't evaluate
in the same way that a scientist evaluates. Perhaps
when we are doing our best it can't be said at all."

Learners who become part of community-based literacy
programs recognize the vision amid the limited resources. Sometimes, this can result in something positive – it can bring out the
best in everyone, especially learners. It can inspire learners to be
more active and to take more responsibility for their program.
And it can inspire them to help other learners and to do more for
themselves.

"The most important thing to me is that I know
myself – where I am and where I want to go. I am
more confident now. I can see more clearly and have
set goals for myself. I started up the ladder and I am
a quarter of the way there. It is a gradual process. It
is hard and it is satisfying.
They say that the race is not for the swift or the
back that is strong, but for those who can do it again.
And that's what I'm doing at the moment. I am doing
it again and again."

Issue: Coping with Growth

## ISSUE: LEARNING TO READ AND WRITE VS. EMPOWERMENT

"Within our program, learners state explicitly that they want to learn to read and write, and they state less explicitly the need for empowerment and social change. For us, this reveals a tension in the mandate of our organization. Are we an educational program or are we a social change program? We expect that if we could be clearer about our purpose, then we could be clearer about what constitutes success."

**How do you know this is an issue for your program?**

"I think that there is a history within community-based literacy programs of having social change and empowerment as a goal. Essentially, we work with people who come from families with low incomes, and hence from disadvantaged backgrounds. It is clear that literacy is not the solution to the problem. At best, it is only a band-aid solution.

The reality is that, even though learners improve their reading and writing skills, it doesn't create great changes in their lives. The real way to make changes is through social change. This view is shared by some people within this organization. Certainly it is shared by staff and some learners and volunteers. We know that there have to be more fundamental changes than simply providing people with opportunities to improve their reading and writing skills. We don't want them to only understand better the letters they get from welfare. And they too want more for themselves than that."

The concept of empowerment is integral to community- based literacy programs, but it presents programs with some difficulties. Partly, this is because it is difficult to know what each program member means by the term empowerment. Not everyone means the same thing when they use the term, and while participants are committed to the concept, they are not even certain themselves what empowerment really looks like for literacy learners.

Some of the questions members grapple with when they use the term empowerment are: is empowerment a goal that can be conceptualized, similar to the way that the acquisition of reading and writing skills can be conceptualized, or is empowerment a process through which reading and writing skills are best learned; or is empowerment a description of the context in which the skills of reading and writing are taught?

Certainly, one of the difficulties is knowing where reading and writing intersects with empowerment, and whether a community-based literacy program that encompasses the notion of empowerment would teach reading and writing differently from a program that does not. It is also a challenge to know whether or not empowerment is occurring. If empowerment is a process, how do learners, volunteers, and staff find indicators that empowerment has occurred?

The issue of reading and writing vs. empowerment is often experienced as a dichotomy, but community-based literacy programs only sometimes experience it in this way. As this issue was addressed, a range of perspectives emerged. There were equally strong feelings that the process of learning to read and write was and was not well integrated with the process of empowerment within the program.

There are moments when the notion of empowerment is challenged, such as when new tutors, learners, or staff join the program and question whether empowerment ought to be part of a literacy program.

> "This [idea of empowerment] is not held by everyone in this organization. We are a community-based program and we welcome a lot of people who do not start from that perspective. There are a lot of learners, volunteers, and board members who come to the program and don't share this perspective."

At other times, learning to read and write is understood as synonymous with empowerment.

> "I think it could be understood differently. While we might all agree that empowerment is fundamental, not everyone has the same notion of how literacy leads to empowerment. Sometimes I feel that we think that the acquisition of reading and writing skills occurs through some magical process – that it will happen by itself and that all you really have to do is concern yourself with how to empower people.
>
> I lead a group with another staff member. He is a very empowering facilitator. He gives the learners all kinds of room to define the curriculum, he encourages discussion, and he is very creative in the way he teaches. And the way I teach is extremely structured. Basically I asked the group what they wanted to know how to do. The majority of this class wanted to learn how to form the letters in cursive, to review their vowel sounds and vowel combinations, and to review basic skills. They wanted to do it long and hard – until they would

never have to feel insecure about writing anything down. And so my notion of empowering these learners was to help them get those skills, and my colleague's notion was to facilitate a different kind of group. In fact, the learners wanted both. When they evaluated his teaching, they said, 'We really like the discussions, but you are not giving us enough literacy skills.' And sometimes they said to me, 'You give us too many drills. You have to lighten up.' There is nothing empowering in and of itself about how to make a perfect capital 'A' in cursive . . . but learners have the right to a basic education in the same way that I did. I don't see that as a conflict – the notion of empowerment and learning to read and write.

Darek Banasik/Canadian Living Magazine

What I want to do is to challenge other people's notions of what empowerment is. I think empowerment can happen when you have good discussion with literacy learners. But I think other people think that empowerment happens when learners start to voice social concerns; when they comment on the world and how it affects them. But every time they learn something, it helps them to do something about their world. And if learning is not happening within the literacy program, then empowerment can't happen. Learning to read and write is empowerment."

Issue: Learning to Read and Write vs. Empowerment

And sometimes, learning to read and write is seen as a first step towards empowerment.

"I think that adult literacy learners who aspire to read and write are people who are aspiring to make changes in their lives. We run a voluntary program – nobody walks in the door for any other reason

other than to make those changes (unless a social worker coerced them into being here, and in that case they will be gone in a few weeks anyway). The learners who stay with the program, which are most of the people who come here, are here because they have aspirations. When they walk through that door they are saying, 'I think this is the road to changing my life,' and then I think we have a starting place for helping social change to happen."

"I am thinking about one learner in particular. I don't think her social position is a whole lot better than it was a couple of years ago, but in many ways it is better. Her social worker has a lot more respect for her, she is linked a lot better to the resources in the community, she knows a lot more about the school system and her kids' routines, and she is proud of herself when she has to write things down publicly. I think that, in spite of the fact that she is still on family benefits and she still lives in this neighbourhood, she has more power than she did two years ago. Now I don't think that this is very earth shaking, but I don't see empowerment as something that happens in a revolutionary way. I see it

ELEMENTS IN INTERACTION

as being slow in Canada – something that
sometimes moves very slowly and yet sometimes
takes jumps."

Some speak of empowerment as synonymous with social
change, and other speak of it as personal growth.

"I have come to understand the notion of empowerment as personal empowerment because most of the
learners here don't really want to discuss social problems. It isn't what they find interesting. They don't
want to talk about what is wrong with the whole
society. If we talked to them about that, then I feel
we would be imposing something on them. It's not
wrong – I certainly see the need for social change,
but somehow I think they are not really interested.
So sometimes I feel discouraged, because there is
this ideal, which I believe in too, but it is just not
related to reality."

"Part of learning to read and write as an adult
involves looking at and thinking about, things in
different ways. Reading and writing can be seen as a
stepping stone to looking more critically at issues. I
think about learners who have been participating in
our program for quite a long time and they really
haven't learned to read and write significantly
better; however, they have made significant changes
in their lives in terms of self-assurance and in terms
of trying new things. It is not to say that they won't
learn to read and write better. It is just that it takes
such a long time, and in truth their literacy skills
haven't progressed at the same rate as other skills,
such as communication."

Issue: Learning to Read and Write vs. Empowerment

Part of the frustration with this issue is the perceived gap between the vision for social change and the day-to-day reality of teaching reading and writing to adult literacy learners.

> "I used to feel sort of jaded about this issue. I still feel it somewhat. There are these ideals in this program about changing things and about giving people skills to read and write so that they could start to take control of their lives. Then, of course, the social structure would start to change because, by empowering the poor, we would be hammering away at the foundations of the establishment. But when you work with learners here day-to-day, it just isn't like that."

Although there were a range of views expressed about the nature of empowerment, an historical survey of the organization's documentation reveals consistent and uninterrupted support for integrating literacy and social change.

> "I was thinking about the long-range planning meeting that we had with volunteers and staff. We got onto the subject of the mandate of this organization. We spent a good couple of hours talking about social change as the foundation for the organization. We looked at our history, which traced the development of this organization as a community-based project that did not see itself as a social-service organization. For us, literacy was not a service that we provided to our clients. Historically, we have rejected the social-service model."

**How does your program respond to this issue?**

ELEMENTS IN INTERACTION

126

The program responds in a range of ways including:

Choosing to present the personal as political:

> "I'm not sure this organization responds to this issue in a consistent way. I don't think it does and I don't think I do either. I think what I try to do is respond to every opportunity in my working life to pick up on an initiative for empowerment that I can, in all good conscience, integrate with literacy.
>
> Let me cite an example from our women's group. The women's group comes out of our broader defini-tion of literacy because it is primarily a discussion group. The goal was to get women to articulate clearly, important issues in their lives. We, as facilitators, of course, had choices about what we could pick up on in the discussion group. We  chose to pick up on the issue that we found was most common to all the women in the group. It was the issue of physical abuse and family separation.
>
> We decided to do a learner-produced story based on that theme. The women were very empowered by that process and by the resource people we had in. These resource people told the learners that it wasn't their fault that they were abused; it was his fault. They needed to hear it over and over again. That is why the book is so important. It was a choice

Issue: Learning to Read and Write vs. Empowerment

127

to do a book for other women who also can't read very well so that they would also hear, over and over again, that it is not their fault, that it was never their fault. That kind of book comes out of a literacy context. But I think we had a choice. We chose to take a political issue and to make that issue public.

I think that the process empowered the learner who produced the story and all the people who participated in producing the book. And I think that the reading of the book by other women who are in literacy programs will be an empowering experience. This is an example of a healthy connection between learning the skills of reading and writing and social change. I don't think any woman's personal/political life is ever the same once she has decided that it was not her fault that she got beaten.

Now that is a minor change, mind you. And even though I too have problems with things moving so slowly, I see changes that are significant and I see my role there as active. There are plenty of places where I don't take an active role, where I simply teach people to be able to print or to write in cursive. I just think that it is really good that they are able to do it and I try to help them. I suppose it isn't really empowering but I like to teach that. There are many other instances when, as a result of my commitment to an empowering process, I assist learners to articulate issues that are important to them and to isolate the instances where we can act."

Increasing learner involvement in the program:

"Through the tutor training, tutors become more aware of learners lives, and learners become more aware of each other. That sensitivity is what makes this a good program."

"The biggest change that we made was to involve learners more in the tutor training. We always try to encourage learners to speak for themselves. Learners have a big impact on the tutors who are first being trained. When learners speak for themselves, tutors listen."

"Learners are used to being seen as clients. It is new for them to be seen as agents of change. Because we have been around for a few years we have a fair amount of learner participation."

**Describe where, in your program, you feel that the issue of learning to read and write vs. empowerment is close to being resolved.**

It is important to grapple with this issue within the context of learners' lives.

"I don't think that this issue is easily resolved. A literacy organization, by its very definition, is not easily an organization for social change. When you start with an issue like literacy you are starting with people who have the least. You have chosen to work with people at the starting point. I don't see the learners in the program as being really conscious of the political issues that underlie the conditions of their lives and as being really active in changing that and doing it in a co-ordinated way with the board of directors. We start with people who have almost nothing in terms of resources and knowledge. We try

Issue: Learning to Read and Write vs. Empowerment

129

to work with them to a point where they can see wider horizons."

Having learners active within a program and involved with issues is considered to be an effective vehicle for empowerment.

"One way is through our involvement in the umbrella organizations. We do advocacy work in clear writing and design that sends out messages to the public that say, 'It is not our learners' fault that they cannot read your message. It is your message that is the problem; it is unreadable.' It is powerful when we see learners advocating for materials that are clearly written. The advocacy work that we do in many areas, with learners speaking for themselves, is very important."

"We have involved the board of directors in advocacy, and we have included learners more effectively in the tutor training. We are trying very hard to bring learners into the decision-making process. We haven't achieved it completely but there is a commitment to try to bring this about. There is a recognition of the value that the learners bring. I was recently at a meeting of the evaluation committee and a learner attended for the first time. The members of the committee thought that it made a significant difference to the committee that he was there."

"The other day I was listening to the radio and one of the learners was on the air speaking about child care. She was so articulate and I was very impressed. There are so many little things that add up to a whole lot – little grains of sand, all moving to build the mountain."

Empowerment is most evident when students participate meaningfully in a range of forums.

ArtWork

"I think the work with the publishing component of this program is really important. Learners are building on the skills they have acquired, whether it is as a result of the clear writing and design consultations they participate in, or being on the board of directors, or sitting on committees, or producing learner-written materials, or participating in tutor training and in tutor workshops, or planning International Literacy Day and speaking at press conferences. A lot of learners are doing a lot. And everyone rallies around learners' accomplishments."

"I am thinking about the learners who produce our magazine. We were talking about education. Suddenly we realized that almost everyone in the group had been labelled mentally retarded. I asked the learners if they still believed that they were mentally retarded. And I asked them if they no longer believed it, at what stage in their lives had they stopped believing it. Many of the learners said that they stopped believing it when they started in this literacy program. It was a real turning point for

Issue: Learning to Read and Write vs. Empowerment

131

them to stop thinking of themselves as mentally retarded. They were able to reflect critically on their parents, social workers, teachers, and adult protective service workers. The learners had decided that these people were wrong about them. For me, that is empowerment."

# *looking forward*

## THE FUTURE OF COMMUNITY-BASED LITERACY

"Maybe in 10 years everything will have hardened
down and they'll have manuals on how to be
community-based, but right now we don't and that's
what makes it so exciting."

Looking back to the late seventies and comparing this period with
the current literacy milieu, we see tremendous growth and development in adult literacy provision. Fifteen years ago in Metro Toronto,
a small number of programs were shaping a relatively new literacy
network. Discussion around literacy tended to focus on such areas as
teaching methodologies and the need to publicize the full scope of
the problem of illiteracy. Programs were influenced by a variety of
approaches such as the work of popular educator Paulo Freire and
the work of Literacy Volunteers of America. Community literacy
work was also influenced by the institutional literacy initiatives,
such as federally funded community college programs, school-based
programs including several adult day schools and a few night classes,

life skills programs, and library reading programs. For the most part, terms such as adult upgrading, adult basic education, and re-entry were used instead of the word literacy.

Fifteen years later, the Metro Toronto literacy scene has changed considerably. There are more programs, more kinds of programs, and they are more visible and better rooted. A flourishing literacy community has resulted in more choices for learners in terms of the kinds of programming, the hours, the locations, and the availability of related services. There are more literacy networks and coalitions and they have become stronger, often reaching out to make links with other social movements, such as the anti-poverty movement. In general, there is a breadth and depth to the literacy movement that did not previously exist.

Community-based literacy programs have played a leading role in this growing and developing adult literacy field. Throughout this fifteen year period, as other adult literacy programs have increased in number and scope, so too have community-based literacy programs. They have matured and become more articulate about their distinct identity within the area of adult literacy provision. Although community-based literacy programs have received a smaller share of the increased financial resources for literacy, they have accomplished a great deal, supplementing these limited resources by drawing on their communities in order to build a participatory community-based literacy movement. Community-based literacy programs have established a progressive educational agenda for their work with literacy learners.

Looking to the future, we anticipate that there will be increasing interest on the part of educators in learning about the nuances of community-based literacy practice. While conducting our research, we were asked whether community-based literacy is a clearly defined practice or model, or whether there is a continuum by which programs might be seen to be more or less based in the community. There is no easy answer to this question. We have suggested that a community-based literacy program is one in which the practice and theory are focused on three elements: learner-centredness, literacy from a critical perspective, and community-building. By presenting this definition, we suggest that a community-based literacy program is based on a distinct practice. If we accept this, then an institutional program, a program with a pre-set curriculum, or one that views literacy as solely an educational problem, would not be considered a community-based literacy program. We have also suggested that community-based literacy programs are developing their practice and theory. This could be interpreted to mean that there is no distinct community-based literacy model, but rather a continuum. In this instance, an institutional program that does not have a community board of directors or volunteers to participate in the community-building process may still operate from a critical perspective and utilize a learner-centred approach. As such, this institutional program might be found somewhere on the continuum of community-based literacy.

In this book, we have shown that community-based literacy has an emerging practice and theory, which is developing in a dynamic way. The theory is developing on a day-to-day basis with people who participate in the programs, but it is not limited to day-to-day practice. When we look into the future of community-based literacy programming, we anticipate that the practice and theory will continue to be shaped and developed.

In particular, we are interested in how the programs will continue to grapple with the three identified elements. It appears to us, as we contemplate the future, that there are contradictions within and among the elements that will have an impact on community-based literacy. Of the three elements, community-building and literacy from a critical perspective might more readily lead to a strengthening of the links between community-based literacy and social change movements. Whereas both community-building and literacy from a critical perspective encourage a collective responsibility for social change, learner-centredness has characteristics that might deflect community-based literacy programs from their social vision. First, learner-centredness is the element that concentrates primarily on the learner within the program rather than the learner within the community. It is the element concerned with developing a learning program that primarily addresses the educational needs of the learner. Second, there is an aspect of learner-centredness that has the possibility of focusing on the individual learner in such a way that, when there are limited resources, the commitment to community may become a secondary concern.

While there are also contradictions between the elements of community-building and literacy from a critical perspective, these contradictions seem to be moving towards a resolution in favour of the commitment to community. The element of community-building for example, when considered in relation to volunteerism, suggests that programs work with the neighbourhood volunteers. Whereas the element of literacy from a critical perspective also suggests a collective or social approach, it critiques the very notion of working with volunteers because of the charitable overtones implicit in the voluntary model. The contradictions between these two elements are becoming better understood in relation to volunteerism. There are indications of a growing confidence about how and why community-based programs work with volunteers. Community-based literacy programs are moving beyond the charitable model of volunteerism and beginning to develop a model in which equality between the tutor and the learner is paramount.

Similarly, in relation to how literacy is defined, literacy from a critical perspective suggests that programs politicize the definition of literacy by bringing to the forefront a socio-economic analysis of literacy and poverty, whereas the element of community-building suggests that this politicization be set aside in order to include everyone in the community regardless of their political perspective. The contradictions between these two elements are also gradually being addressed. There is a greater emphasis on listening to learners speak about the realities of their lives. The authenticity of the learners' voices speaking about poverty from their experiences enables program members to develop a deeper understanding of literacy and poverty. This promotes collective discussion and united action around these issues.

Again, it appears that tensions around the element of learner-centredness may be less easily resolved. While there have been tensions between the other two elements, these are being addressed in such a way that the integrity of both elements is maintained. However, the significant contradiction between the element of learner-centredness and the other two elements may challenge the integrity of the element of learner-centredness. In relation to collective responsibility for social change, community-building and literacy from a critical perspective suggest that programs emphasize group-building and a collective student role in advocacy. On the other hand, learner-centredness suggests that programs provide individualized, one-to-one instruction, based on the needs of learners.

As programs opt for more group work, it becomes difficult to achieve learner-centredness in practice. For example, practitioners complain of the difficulties experienced when trying to meet each learner's needs within a group and learners complain about the challenges of working together with other learners. There is also, in theory, an inherent contradiction within learner-centredness because it does not necessarily situate the student within a social context. For example, in relation to learners' stories, the element of learner-centeredness suggests that programs promote the publishing of students' writings. While the approach is a learner-centred one and may be compatible with the other two elements, sometimes students' writings only further the interests of one learner at the expense of the community of learners, such as when students' writings reflect the conservative motif that "anyone can succeed if they only try hard enough." In these cases, learners' stories do not further the critical motif that there is a social factor in the achievement of individual success.

The elements of community-building and literacy from a critical perspective are the ones that we anticipate will continue to develop in important ways, shaping a community-based literacy practice that will support social change. Alternately, the role of learner-centredness may provide a greater challenge to community-based literacy. As community-based literacy programs become more connected to social change movements and more involved in collective action, there is a risk that learner-centredness may become diffused. Given the significance of learner-centredness to community-based literacy practice and theory, we hope that programs will explore the full potential of this element. We wonder if learner-centredness might be transformed to become more compatible with the critical and community-building elements, and with the premise that people both shape, and are shaped by, society. Because learner-centredness is so integral to community-based literacy, both in terms of one-to-one tutoring and responding to learners' needs, we are hopeful that community-based programs will find a way to maintain the integrity of this element.

This book ends the way it began, with a dream of a better world and with a commitment to honour the hopes and educational aspirations of people who are given the least in our society. The creative energy and social commitment within community-based literacy will continue to move the dream forward. The willingness to struggle for a just society is the legacy and the future of community-based literacy.

# FACT SHEETS

## East End Literacy

**Name of program:** Toronto East End Literacy Project

**Office(s):**  265 Gerrard Street East
Toronto, Ontario
M5A 2G3
(416) 968-6989

**Facility:**  East End Literacy is located in rent-free premises on the
second floor of the Parliament Street Library House
owned by the Toronto Public Library.

**Name of community/communities and boundaries:**
The communities served by East End Literacy are wards 6
to 10 of the City of Toronto. The borders are Yonge Street
on the west, Scarborough on the east, Danforth Avenue
on the north, and Lake Ontario on the south.

**Size of Community:**  Population approximately 200,000

**Co-operates closely with:**  Literacy programs throughout Metro
Toronto and Ontario, especially Parkdale Project READ,
St. Christopher House Literacy Project, and ALFA in

Toronto; ALSO in Ottawa; Action Read in Guelph; and CORE Literacy in Kitchener. East End Literacy is active in the Metro Toronto Movement for Literacy and in the Ontario Literacy Coalition. Close co-operation exists between East End Literacy and the Toronto Board of Education and the Toronto Public Library. Close contact is also maintained with Neighbourhood Information Post, Central Neighbourhood House, Dixon Hall, community health centres and organizations within Regent Park.

**Program initiated by:** The program was initiated by three community workers in co-operation with the Regent Park Residents' Association and received initial funding from organizations such as Downtown Churchworkers' Association, PLURA (Presbyterian, Lutheran, United, Roman Catholic, and Anglican churches), and the Children's Aid Society Foundation.

**Full-time staff:** 5

**Part-time staff:** None

**Student/tutor pairs:** 75

**Small groups:** There are three permanent groups. Short-term groups, from eight to ten weeks in duration, are initiated periodically in response to interest.

**Board composition:** 18 elected members and 2 staff representatives

**1988 Annual Budget:** $206,000

**Major Funding Sources:**

|  | % |
|---|---|
| Federal government | 3.2 |
| Provincial government | 36.4 |
| Municipal government | 1.2 |
| Board(s) of education | 26.5 |
| Foundations | 12.1 |
| Other | 20.6 |

## Peel Literacy Guild

**Name of program:** The Peel Literacy Guild Inc.

**Office(s):** 93 Dundas St. East          118 Queen St. West
Suite 105                      Suite 302
Mississauga, Ontario           Brampton, Ontario
L5A 1W7                        L6X 1A4
(416) 273-5196                 (416) 454-3982

**Facility:**    The newly refurbished Mississauga Tutoring Centre is located on the second floor of a strip mall close to one of the busiest intersections in Mississauga and easily accessible by public transit. Seven private tutoring cubicles and one large group room are available in the daytime. In the evening, when staff work areas are free, an additional four spaces are available. Parking is plentiful and free of charge. Hours of operation are: Monday to Thursday 9:00 a.m. to 9:00 p.m. and Friday 9:00 a.m. to 1:00 p.m.

A second office, the Brampton Tutoring Centre, is situated two blocks west of the Four Corners (Brampton Centre) in a three-storey office building that is wheelchair accessible. The office has an abundance of natural light and the atmosphere is very pleasant. Public transit and free parking are available. During the day, six cubicles and one large group room are available for tutoring, and in the evening, eight cubicles and one large group room are available.

Both centres have literacy resource libraries and displays for both learners and tutors. In addition, the availability of free coffee encourages learners and tutors to stay and chat among themselves as well as with staff.

Space at both locations is rented at market rates. No donated space is available due to the growth in the region.

**Name of community/communities and boundaries:**
The Peel Literacy Guild covers all of the Region of Peel.
This area extends from Etobicoke Creek in the east to the
Region of Halton (Oakville) in the west, and from Lake
Ontario on the south to Dufferin County (Orangeville) in
the north. The major centres include Mississauga,
Brampton, and Caledon.

**Size of Community:** 1257 square kilometres/454 square miles;
Population approximately 630,000

**Co-operates closely with:** The Brampton Public Library, Community
Living Mississauga, the Dufferin-Peel Separate School
Board, Ontario Ministry of Correctional Services, Ontario
Ministry of Community Legal Services, Mississauga Day
Hospital, Mississauga Library System, Peel Social
Services, Sheridan College, the Peel Board of Education,
the Town of Caledon Public Library, Youth Employment
Services.

**Program initiated by:** The program was initiated by the Dufferin-
Peel Roman Catholic Separate School Board and the
Mississauga Library with funds from Canada Employment
and Immigration.

**Full-time staff:** 4

**Part-time staff:** 4

**Student/tutor pairs:** 217

**Small groups:** 11

APPENDIX A

**Board composition:** 25 board members, including elected members and appointed representatives

**1988 Annual Budget:** $270,300

> Note: Of this total amount, $152,300 (57%) is the operating budget of the Peel Literacy Guild and the balance (43%) is a direct contribution of the Peel Board of Education.

**Major Funding Sources:**

|  | % |
|---|---|
| Federal government | 33 |
| Provincial government | 45 |
| Municipal government | 0 |
| Board(s) of education | * |
| Foundations | 3 |
| Other (bingo games, donations) | 19 |

* This does not include the contribution made by the Peel Board of Education.

# ALFA

**Name of program:** Toronto Adult Literacy for Action Centre (ALFA)

**Office(s):** 1900 Davenport Road
Toronto, Ontario
M6N 1B7
(416) 652-3652

**Facility:** ALFA is located in the Davenport-Perth Neighbourhood Centre and pays a monthly rent of $500.

**Name of community/communities and boundaries:**
ALFA is bordered by Bloor Street to the south, Christie Street to the east and the City of Toronto boundaries to the north and west. It includes the district of Davenport and the northwest section of the district of High Park.

**Size of Community:** Population approximately 80,580

**Co-operates closely with:** Davenport-Perth Neighbourhood Centre, the Toronto Board of Education, the Toronto Public Library, the Metro Toronto Movement for Literacy, and the Davenport-High Park Network.

**Program Initiated by:** ALFA was started by West End Literacy, a coalition of groups and individuals concerned with adult literacy and community development in the west end of Toronto. During 1984, the coalition worked to establish ALFA, and by the end of 1985 the program was in place.

**Full-time staff:** 3

**Part-time staff:** 1

Student/tutor pairs:  35

Small groups:   2

Board composition:  10

1988 Annual Budget:  $125,000

Major Funding Sources:

|  | % |
|---|---|
| Federal government | 0 |
| Provincial government | 29 |
| Municipal government | 12 |
| Board(s) of education | 20 |
| Foundations | 8 |
| Other | 31 |

# SUMMARY OF THE
# RESEARCH PROCESS

## 1. Overview

The purpose of the study was to provide a forum for community-based literacy program participants to meet together to discuss and learn about community-based literacy, and, through this process, to document and analyze community-based literacy as it is being practised in the greater Metropolitan Toronto area.

The idea for this study originated with the Participatory Research Group (PRG). During 1984-86, the PRG literacy advisory committee met to develop a proposal and explore funding possibilities. In 1987, when funding was secured from the Maytree Foundation and the Ontario government , the research study was formally launched. The volunteer Project Working Group, consisting of a representative of PRG and two members from local community-based literacy programs, was formed to co-ordinate the project. Subsequently, in the summer of 1987, Elaine Gaber-Katz and Gladys Watson were chosen by the Project Working Group to be the researchers for the project. The working group felt that, given the researchers' experience with and commitment to community-based literacy, they would be trusted by community-based literacy programs to conduct the research in a sensitive manner.

The working group wanted the project to follow a participatory process, which would actively involve learners as well as program volunteers and staff in the research. The researchers were asked to conduct the study using a participatory and consultative research methodology. The working group anticipated that the final product would document the nature of community-based literacy programming, and that the participatory process would also support the development of community-based literacy practice.

## 2. Methodology

In keeping with the participatory research methodology, the researchers set up a project design, which involved three community-based literacy programs in the Metro Toronto area.

Early in the study, programs were asked to comment on the project design, including the content of the agendas for the proposed research meetings. Throughout the research process, staff, board members, volunteers, and learners from each of the three designated programs participated actively in the research discussions. Each participant was given the opportunity to make suggestions regarding the content and format of the final report. Also, each participant was invited to review the draft report and to give comments before the report was finalized. At this stage, however, some of the learners who had participated could not be located. Consequently, input by these learners was limited to their participation in the research meetings.

Since community-based literacy is evolving, participants wanted a research report that would reflect the developing nature of the practice. They asked that the resulting book reflect the divergent opinions that are sometimes present in the community-based literacy movement. They also asked that the book pursue an analysis of community-based literacy. For example, one of the strong recommendations from program participants was that the book be more than description and quotes. Participants in the study urged the researchers to go beyond what had been learned at the research meetings by analyzing the data to draw out new insights and conclusions. At the same time, participants wanted the book to capture the process and reflect the collective nature of the research.

### 3. Project Timeline

The project took place over a period of approximately four years, from its formative stages in 1986 to the production of the book in 1990. Throughout this period, everyone including the two researchers was involved in the project on a part-time basis.

The project was organized into several phases:

Project planning and design (June 1987 - November 1987)
- meetings with the working group
- project design
- identification of programs
- consultation with programs regarding project design

Data collection (November 1987 - March 1988)
- two research meetings with each of the three programs
- weekend retreat with the three programs and the working group
- call for printed information and documentation from the three programs, which were the case studies, and from ten other literacy programs that were operating in the Metropolitan Toronto area at the time the study commenced
- transcription of tapes from research meetings

Review and analysis of data (April 1988 - August 1988)
- detailed review and analysis of all transcripts
- meetings with working group to interpret data

Writing (September 1988 - April 1989)
- initial draft of book (research report)

Participants' review of draft (April 1989 - May 1989)

- ◆ draft circulated to each participant within the three programs and to members of the working group

Final draft (June 1989 - December 1989)

Production (1990)

- ◆ photographs of programs

## 4. Choosing the Programs

The researchers faced a dilemma when selecting the community-based literacy programs to participate in the study. They needed to identify, in the absence of a definition of community-based literacy, which programs were, in fact, community-based literacy programs. They began by asking questions of themselves and others. Are all literacy programs that call themselves community-based literacy programs really community-based literacy programs? If not, then who should make the decision as to which programs should be called community-based literacy programs?

In the face of these difficult questions, the researchers established criteria to select three programs from those that were relying on their community in their ongoing operation. Each of the programs chosen was to have an independent board of directors. As well, a combination of other factors were considered. Programs were to be either independent or part of a larger community organization, such as a library or community centre. Programs were to represent a range of geographic communities within greater Metropolitan Toronto (west, central, and east). Both new and old programs were to be included. Also, programs with different staffing models – a hierarchical structure with a supervisor and a collective structure – were to be part of the study.

The researchers limited the study to three programs because there were only enough financial resources to study three programs in-depth. At the time of the study, only thirteen self-identified community-based literacy programs existed in the Metro Toronto area. Three out of thirteen was deemed to be a reasonable sample.

It should be noted that other programs could have illustrated community-based literacy equally as well as the three that were chosen. All of these programs have influenced the study in the sense that much of the understanding that the researchers have about community-based literacy was derived from their experience of community-based literacy in Metro Toronto and the contributions that all of these programs have made to the community-based literacy movement.

## 5. Data Collection

Data was gathered from two groups of programs – from the three literacy programs that were chosen as the case studies for the project, and from the remaining ten literacy programs located in the greater Metropolitan Toronto area at the time the study began. While the ten programs were notified about the study and asked to provide information about their programs including printed documentation (see Appendix C), the main source of data was the three case studies. These three programs provided a wealth of data for the project, primarily through research meetings, which were taped and transcribed. The data collection process used with the three programs is described below.

A letter was sent to East End Literacy, the Peel Literacy Guild, and ALFA asking each program to choose a staff contact person and other staff, volunteer tutors, board members, and learners who would be interested in participating in the project. Each program did so and representatives then participated in two evening research meetings that focused on information about their program. The program participants from all three programs then gathered for a weekend retreat to discuss, describe, and analyze community-based literacy. In recognition of the considerable time and resources that the programs committed to the project, an honorarium was paid to each program.

## Interview Questions

### Interview questions from the first round of research meetings

a. Description

How do you define a community-based literacy program?
How are community-based literacy programs organized?
What are the different components of a community-based literacy program?

- Describe the organizational, staff, and program structure.
- Describe the curriculum and the methodology used.
- Who are the participants – staff, volunteers, learners, board, community (in terms of their background, socio-economic characteristics, hopes, concerns, etc.)?

What distinguishes community-based literacy programs from other literacy/adult education programs, social service organizations, and other educational institutions (e.g., the elementary school that these adults may have attended previously)?

b. Goals

What are the goals of community-based literacy work?
Are there any gaps between the goals and what actually takes place:

- between what is taught to the learners and what is learned by the learners?
- between what is taught to the volunteer tutors and what the tutors teach the learners?

c. Dilemmas

There are dilemmas and tensions within community-based literacy work. What is your understanding of how the following dilemmas and tensions affect community-based literacy programs?

- the use of one-to-one teaching/the use of group teaching;
- the use of volunteers/the demand for public funds for literacy education;
- the merits of a curriculum designed for learners by learners/the merits of a curriculum designed for learners by educators;
- the acquisition of critical skills/the acquisition of functional skills;
- the desire to deliver a high-quality program/the desire to deliver a program that reaches greater numbers of people;
- the desire to participate in building the literacy movement/the desire to respond to the needs within the program;
- organic growth arising from learners' needs/planning in response to available funding;
- learner involvement in decision-making/the nature and demands of decision-making within programs;
- balancing the needs of learners, the needs of staff, the needs of volunteers, the needs of community, and the needs of funders;
- accountability for literacy education through the public education system/accountability for literacy education through the local community;
- the importance of learning to read and write/the importance of empowerment or social change;
- understanding illiteracy as an individual problem/understanding illiteracy as a social problem;
- understanding illiteracy as a Canadian problem/understanding illiteracy as an immigrant problem.

### Interview questions from the second round of research meetings

The participants identified an issue that they felt was most relevant to their particular program from the list of dilemmas presented at the first research meeting, and addressed the following questions, as follows:

- What happens within your program that leads you as a group to identify this issue?
- How does your program respond to this issue?
- Where in your program do you feel that this issue is close to being resolved?

### Agenda and questions from the weekend retreat

The retreat was held on a Friday evening and all day Saturday. On the Friday evening, the session was informal. Three small group discussions were held around the following questions.

- Why are we all involved in community-based literacy?
- What attracted you to the program you are in?
- What makes you stay?

On the Saturday morning, the session began with a discussion of what each of the following terms mean to participants:

- Learner-Centred
- Literacy
- Community

On the Saturday afternoon, the session focused on:

- Looking forward to the future of community-based literacy

## 6. List of Participants*

**ALFA**

Christine Almeida (Staff)
Tannis Atkinson (Staff and Project Contact Person)
Gwen Davies (Staff)
Jude Dawes (Board Member)
Brenda Duncombe (Board Member)
Josephine Hines (Learner)
Paul Simpson (Learner)
Donna Zwolak (Board Member and Tutor)

**East End Literacy**

Betsy Alkenbrack (Staff and Project Contact Person)
Karen Diver (Board Member)
Sally McBeth (Staff)
Elaine Sims (Learner)
Ruth Wehlau (Board Member)

**Peel Literacy Guild**

Elva Duff (Tutor)
Heather Hufton (Staff and Project Contact Person)
Nancy Moura (Staff)
Trudy Reid (Learner)
Grace Scheel (Board Member)
Wally Ward (Board Member)

* This research study took more than four years to complete. During this time some of the staff members, learners, and tutors who participated in the study left their programs. Nonetheless, all of the participants listed above attended all of the research meetings, except for Paul Simpson from A L F A and Elaine Sims from East End Literacy, who attended two out of three sessions. Most of the program participants reviewed drafts of the book and submitted comments and suggestions.

# PROFILES OF
# LITERACY PROGRAMS
# IN METRO TORONTO

In 1987, there were thirteen adult literacy programs in Metropolitan Toronto considered by the Ontario Government, for funding purposes, to be community-based literacy programs. Most of these programs, initiated by community advocates, began modestly as small, one-to-one volunteer tutoring programs.

For the most part, these community literacy programs receive their direction from community boards or advisory bodies, with the exception of programs such as Frontier College, a large national literacy organization, which has its head office in Toronto, and Adult Literacy York (ALY), a program which was initiated by the York Board of Education. Community affiliation – with boards of education, public libraries, and community agencies – is integral to the ongoing operation of most of these programs.

Usually, community literacy programs adopt an informal assessment process in which learners actively participate. Learners begin by setting their own learning plans, which contain their educational goals. At a later date, the plans are reviewed by learners with the assistance of staff and volunteer tutors.

Many of these literacy programs use a learner-centred approach in which the curriculum is closely tied to the learners' stated goals. In these instances, volunteer tutors participate in a training program that prepares them for teaching reading and writing, usually applying whole language theory and using the language experience method. The context for teaching reading and writing is the community context; hence, community resources and community research form part of the curriculum for learners.

Community literacy programs are free of charge for adult learners. Most programs strive to undertake, with limited funding, a range of programming, which may include one-to-one and group tutoring; student publishing; leadership development; public education on the issue of literacy; advocacy; networking; and volunteer development. Funding comes from a range of sources, such as the Ontario Government, local boards of education, private foundations, local municipal grants, the United Way of Greater Toronto, service clubs, churches, and special fundraising events such as book sales and bingo games.

### Toronto Adult Literacy for Action Centre (ALFA)*

ALFA, one of the newer literacy programs in Toronto, is located in the northwestern end of the city. It was initiated in 1985 by West End Literacy – a coalition of groups and individuals concerned with adult literacy and community development in the west end of Toronto.

Located in the Davenport-Perth United Church, ALFA is a tenant of the Davenport-Perth Neighbourhood Centre, a multi-service community centre. ALFA's board of directors is drawn from the community and supports the activities of four staff members working with thirty-five learner/tutor pairs.

Community education on the issue of literacy is important to ALFA, whose staff and volunteers are active in the Metro Toronto Movement for Literacy (MTML); the Toronto Public Library's literacy committee; and other provincial and national organizations concerned with literacy. While financial concerns sometimes preoccupy ALFA, their involvement with the community newspaper, *Neighbours,* and the assistance they lend to other community literacy efforts, such as helping to start the Bloor/Gladstone Library literacy program, reflect the community context in which ALFA operates.

### Adult Literacy York (ALY)

In 1985, the Board of Education for the City of York, a small municipality to the north of the City of Toronto, received a federal job-creation grant that allowed them to launch Adult Literacy York. When this grant funding ended, the York Board of Education began to offer literacy, English as a Second Language, and upgrading programs through the school system, using paid teachers who held Ontario Teachers' Certificates.

Adult Literacy York is a very large program, operating out of several elementary and secondary schools, and employing a large number of teachers. This program views itself as a school-based literacy program. One unique feature of Adult Literacy York is the one-to-one tutorial outreach program, which enables learners to receive private instruction in their own homes through tutoring sessions with visiting teachers.

### Alexandra Park Learning Centre

Alexandra Park Learning Centre is located in a large public housing complex in downtown Toronto. In 1985, residents combined forces with the Alexandra Park Residents' Association, community workers, and staff from the local school to initiate this small program, which is located in a townhouse in the Alexandra Park housing project.

Alexandra Park Learning Centre offers a tutoring program in adult basic literacy; English as a Second Language; upgrading in reading, writing, spelling, and math; and a children's homework program. In addition, this program provides educational referral and counselling, and a typing class.

The innovative feature of this program is that it works closely with a community residents' association, offering many possibilities for integrating literacy effectively into community life. Although there are some tensions as the residents' association and the literacy program strive to sort out their individual mandates and establish a more effective organizational structure, Alexandra Park Learning Centre is in an excellent position to promote itself as a "place for living and a place for learning" because it can

APPENDIX C

naturally integrate literacy with community activities.

### Bloor/Gladstone Public Library Literacy Program

As a branch initiative of the Bloor/Gladstone Public Library, a literacy tutoring program was started in 1986, with assistance from ALFA and Parkdale Project READ – two literacy programs in the west end of Toronto. The library community-liaison worker is responsible for the branch literacy tutoring program, co-ordinating four learner/tutor pairs.

The Bloor/Gladstone Branch Library has a commitment to literacy and participates in various forums on literacy within the Toronto Public Library.

### East End Literacy*

Initiated by community workers in 1978, East End Literacy is a one-to-one and small group tutoring program. Located in an old Victorian library house owned by the Parliament Street Library, East End Literacy works primarily with English-speaking learners who live in the east end of Toronto. East End Literacy has seventy-five learner/ tutor pairs who meet either in the community or the reading centre operated by the program.

Community education, advocacy, and clear writing and design are integral to East End Literacy's programming. East End Literacy is perhaps best known for its publishing. East End Literacy Press has produced a number of publications including the *Writer's Voice*, a student-written and student-produced periodical and the *New Start Reading Series*, a series of books produced for adult new readers. In addition, East End Literacy is known for its pioneering work in the area of student leadership and student involvement.

East End Literacy has a strong board of directors that supports a staff of five literacy workers. Active participation in local, provincial, and national literacy organizations is a priority for East End Literacy. While this program has chosen to remain a small, local literacy program that provides literacy learners with a community educational alternative, it assists other community literacy programs to get started. East End Literacy has conducted several program evaluations and has thoroughly documented its development as a community-based literacy program.

### East York Learning Experience

East York Learning Experience is a new literacy program that has just completed a two-year developmental phase. Located in East York, Metropolitan Toronto's only borough, this literacy program was a community-development initiative of East End Literacy. Started in 1984, the East York Learning Experience has become an independent program with its own board of directors drawn from the local community.

Like other literacy programs, this program operates with multi-based funding. In a manner consistent with this borough, community support for the program is strong, including the East York Public Library, Community Care, the Lions' Club, the East York Development Council, and the East York Board of Education.

With twenty-two learning pairs, the East York Learning Experience trains volunteer tutors to work one-to-one or in small groups with adults who want to develop or improve skills in reading, writing, and math. The East York Learning Experience is also concerned about the rapid expansion of their program within the context of limited resources for literacy.

### Frontier College

Frontier College is a large, national organization, which co-ordinates a range of programs: Literacy in the Workplace, Prison Literacy, Independent Studies, Beat the Street, and the Help Program. The organization has an independent board of directors that includes several prominent Canadians.

Frontier College has a long history of providing adult education in isolated, rural areas of Canada. In the late 1970s, however, it underwent a major programming shift – from working in the frontiers across the country to working in urban settings. Frontier College is known in literacy circles for the development of the SCIL program – a program used to "determine the immediate needs of a student, and to develop a suitable curriculum based on those needs." While offering programs in the Toronto area, Frontier College does not draw upon a specific geographic community in the way that the other literacy programs do. It is primarily active in advocacy for literacy at the national level.

Recently Frontier College established the Frontier College Learning Foundation to raise money for literacy by means of an independent trust fund. The Foundation provides "the means for the college to initiate vital research and program development that cannot be marketed to more traditional funding bodies."

### North York Public Library Literacy Program

The North York Public Library Literacy Program, a library-based literacy program, which was one of the first programs in the Metro Toronto area, has provided leadership and inspiration to many fledgling literacy programs within Toronto and throughout the province of Ontario. Started in 1977 in the City of North York, the program has offices in several library branches and employs four full-time staff. From time-to-time, additional part-time staff is hired, usually with funding obtained by short-term project grants.

The North York Literacy Program, with a larger student-staff ratio than many of the other literacy programs in Toronto, worked with three hundred and eighty learners during 1988. Primarily a one-to-one tutoring program, the North York Literacy Program also works with special needs groups such as intellectually handicapped adults, and offers a range of programs such as life skills, crafts, and reading and spelling groups. One unique feature of this program is its computer centre, which is very popular with learners and tutors.

Active in numerous literacy networks and coalitions, the North York Literacy Program often sponsors conferences, workshops, and other literacy events. One of the challenges faced by this program is the struggle to become more of a community literacy program – a goal sometimes difficult to attain within a large institution.

### Parkdale Project READ

Parkdale Project READ is a well-established literacy program in the west end of Toronto. Initiated in 1980 by a community-oriented librarian at the Parkdale Public Library, Parkdale Project READ is an interesting model of a public library's initiative resulting in the creation of a community-based literacy program rather than a library-based literacy program. The board of directors of Parkdale Project READ is an independent board with membership drawn from learners, tutors, staff, board of education representatives, Parkdale Library representatives, and other interested community members.

Located in a vibrant and diverse neighbourhood, Parkdale Project READ has initiated community education projects in the area of clear language and design for community and national organizations on such matters as health, housing, and legal rights. In keeping with its strong community focus, Parkdale Project READ helped to start other literacy programs such as ALFA and the Bloor/Gladstone Library Program. Parkdale Project READ has also assisted other organizations interested in literacy, such as the Metro Toronto Association for Community Living.

Interested in promoting the publication of students' writings as an important aspect of literacy work, Parkdale Project READ annually publishes *Parkdale Writes*, a collection of learners' writings, and has published *My Story* by Olive Bernard in collaboration with Toronto Public Library. Parkdale Project READ describes itself as using a learner-based approach to adult education, which fosters self-direction in the learning process. Active in literacy networks and coalitions, the program regards advocacy as an important part of its work. Although the community is central to Parkdale Project READ, this program is very cognizant of the "cost" involved in integrating literacy work with community, given the lack of funding available to literacy groups that support an authentic community process.

### Peel Literacy Guild*

The Peel Literacy Guild began in 1981 and currently has two tutoring centres, one in the City of Mississauga and one in the City of Brampton. The region of Peel is not officially part of Metropolitan Toronto, but it is considered part of "greater Metro." The cities of Mississauga and Brampton cover large geographic areas and have a growing and changing population, making the development of a community literacy program a challenge.

The Peel Literacy Guild, starting with funds from a federal grant, developed a funding strategy, which now enables them to draw funding from a range of sources, including private foundations, fundraising events such as bingo games, and government grants. Firmly rooted in its community, the Peel Literacy Guild enjoys the support of many community agencies and institutions, including both the separate and the public boards of education, the Mississauga Library system, and various service clubs and churches.

Currently working with over two hundred and seventeen learners, the Peel Literacy Guild publishes several student-written publications and prepares for its tutors, some of whom are paid, creative packages that facilitate the teaching of basic skills. Peel Literacy Guild is very active in literacy networks and has been, and continues to be, a strong supporter of the Metro Toronto Movement for Literacy.

### St. Christopher House Literacy Program

With a mandate to provide literacy programming in the central area of Toronto since the late 1970s, the St. Christopher House Literacy Program offers one-to-one and small group tutoring. In addition, they organize English as a Second Language Literacy classes, in co-operation with the Toronto Board of Education. The St.

Christopher House Literacy Program is one of the few literacy centres that also offer mother-tongue literacy classes.

This interest in mother-tongue literacy, coupled with the support and counsel of various ethno-cultural groups within the community, led the program to assist in the development of the Multilingual Literacy Centre. Recently, the centre became incorporated as an independent literacy organization, although it still maintains close ties with the St. Christopher House Literacy Program.

The St. Christopher House Literacy Program is a meeting place for forty-five learner/tutor pairs. The literacy program is only one of the many programs offered by St. Christopher House, a well-established settlement house. Working within a unionized workplace, five staff co-ordinate more than one hundred literacy learners and over ninety volunteers.

### St. George's Adult Literacy Program
Working in the north Toronto area, the St. George's Adult Literacy Program co-ordinates twenty learning pairs. Primarily funded by the Toronto Board of Education, leadership for this fairly new literacy program comes from the active volunteers of St. George's United Church.

The St. George's Adult Literacy Program began as a pilot project, drawing tutors from church volunteers. It received support from several literacy programs and organizations such as the North York Adult Literacy Program, ALFA, the Scarborough Adult Basic Literacy Program, the Orchard View Branch of Toronto Public Library and the Adult Basic Education Unit of the Toronto Board of Education.

Seeking funds for a full-time staff co-ordinator, the St. George's Adult Literacy Program is struggling to move beyond the developmental phase to become a full-fledged literacy program.

### Scarborough Adult Basic Literacy
In 1982, with a mandate to serve the City of Scarborough, to the

east of the City of Toronto, the Scarborough Adult Basic Literacy program began with an advisory board consisting of staff, volunteers, and church members. This program is sponsored by the Scarborough Board of Education in co-operation with Metro Toronto Department of Community Services, and space is provided by the Washington United Church.

Working with ninety learning pairs, this program makes a commitment to appreciate the rich resources that each individual person brings to the program, including differences in dialect and culture; the linguistic competence of each learner and a commitment to build on this competence; the active involvement of students in the selection of materials and in the decisions as to what is to be learned; and finally, the different speeds at which individual students learn.

The Adult Basic Literacy program is active in the Metro Toronto Movement for Literacy and has hosted several conferences and workshops for the Metro Toronto literacy community. This program, committed to a student-centered curriculum, publishes a student-written periodical entitled *My Word.*

\* ALFA, East End Literacy, and Peel Literacy Guild were the case studies for this research project.

APPENDIX C

# LIST OF LITERACY PROGRAMS IN
# METRO TORONTO

This is a list of the adult literacy programs in Metropolitan Toronto that have been funded by the Ontario Ministry of Skills Development as community-based literacy programs. The addresses are current as of the time of research.

| Name | Address | Phone |
|------|---------|-------|
| Toronto Adult Literacy For Action Centre (ALFA) | 1900 Davenport Road Toronto, Ontario M6N 1B7 | 652-3652 |
| Adult Literacy York (ALY) | 300 Caledonia Road Room 7 Toronto, Ontario M6E 4T5 | 394-2295 |
| Alexandra Park Learning Centre | 101 Denison Avenue Toronto, Ontario M5A 1N1 | 591-7384 |
| Bloor/Gladstone Public Library Literacy Program | 1101 Bloor St. West Toronto, Ontario M6A 1M7 | 393-7674 |

| | | |
|---|---|---|
| East End Literacy | 265 Gerrard St. East<br>Toronto, Ontario<br>M5A 2G3 | 968-6989 |
| East York Learning<br>Experience | 2085 Danforth Avenue<br>Toronto, Ontario<br>M4C 1K1 | 467-7800 |
| Frontier College | 35 Jackes Avenue<br>Toronto, Ontario<br>M4T 1E2 | 923-3591 |
| North York Public<br>Library Literacy Program | 5120 Yonge Street<br>Willowdale, Ontario<br>M2N 5N7 | 733-5552 |
| Parkdale Project READ | 1303 Queen St. West<br>Toronto, Ontario<br>M6K 1L7 | 531-6308 |
| Peel Literacy Guild | 93 Dundas St. East<br>Suite 105<br>Mississauga, Ontario<br>L5A 1W7 | 273-5196 |
| St. Christopher House<br>Literacy Program | 248 Ossington Avenue<br>Toronto, Ontario<br>M6J 3A2 | 539-9000 |
| St. George's Adult<br>Literacy Program | 35 Lytton Blvd.<br>Toronto, Ontario<br>M4R 1L2 | 484-3736 |

| | | |
|---|---|---|
| Scarborough Adult Basic Literacy | c/o Washington United Church | 267-8362 |
| | 3739 Kingston Road | |
| | Scarborough, Ontario | |
| | M1J 3H4 | |

# WORKSHOP TOOL

In this appendix, the elements of community-based literacy are presented in "hand-out" format so that they may be reproduced for discussion groups and workshops, and for other similar educational purposes.

# THE ELEMENTS OF COMMUNITY-BASED LITERACY

The elements of community-based literacy are:

- learner-centredness;
- literacy from a critical perspective;
- community-building.

Source: Gaber-Katz, Elaine and Gladys M. Watson. *The Land that We Dream of . . . A Participatory Study of Community-Based Literacy.* Toronto: OISE Press, 1991.

# LEARNER-
# CENTREDNESS

Within community-based literacy programs, **learner-centredness** means that programs:

- listen to literacy learners and elicit stories about their lives;
- believe that everyone can learn;
- emphasize equality among learners, volunteers, and staff;
- encourage learners to become involved, both in the program and in the community;
- ensure that learning will be relevant;
- provide a range of programming options;
- assist learners in setting their own learning goals and measuring their own progress;
- ensure that learners' interests and needs determine the curriculum.

Source: Gaber-Katz, Elaine and Gladys M. Watson. *The Land that We Dream of . . . A Participatory Study of Community-Based Literacy.* Toronto: OISE Press, 1991.

# LITERACY FROM A CRITICAL PERSPECTIVE

In community-based literacy programs, **literacy from a critical perspective** means that programs assist learners to:

- improve their basic skills in reading, writing, numeracy, communication, life skills, abstract thinking, and general knowledge;
- increase their critical abilities;
- build self-confidence;
- increase their understanding of self;
- participate more fully in society;
- create language and culture;
- enhance the quality of their own lives;
- work towards empowerment and social change.

Source: Gaber-Katz, Elaine and Gladys M. Watson. *The Land that We Dream of . . . A Participatory Study of Community-Based Literacy.* Toronto: OISE Press, 1991.

# COMMUNITY-
# BUILDING

In community-based literacy, **community-building** means that programs:

- are located in the community at convenient locations, are open at convenient times, are responsive to community needs, and co-operate closely with other neighbourhood services;
- foster the development of common interests and goals;
- encourage literacy to be understood and practised as a social process;
- create a sense of belonging;
- draw upon members of the community to share responsibility for the education of other adults within the community;
- help learners to acquire an understanding of self in relation to society;
- work to build supportive communities.

Source: Gaber-Katz, Elaine and Gladys M. Watson. *The Land that We Dream of . . . A Participatory Study of Community-Based Literacy.* Toronto: OISE Press, 1991.

# NOTES

1. Excerpt from "Somewhere over the Rainbow." Arlen, Harold in David Bickman, ed. *The Harold Arlen Songbook.* United States: MPL Communications; Winona, MN; Milwaukee, WI. Exclusively distributed by Hal Leonard Pub. Corp., 1985.

2. Thomas, Audrey. *Adult Illiteracy in Canada: A Challenge. Canadian Commission for Unesco Occasional Paper no. 42.* Ottawa: Canadian Commission for Unesco, summer 1983.

   The use of statistics to describe the scope of the literacy problem in Canada is controversial. We have chosen not to cite statistics. Those readers interested in a statistical analysis of illiteracy in Canada may turn to several recent studies, as well as the earlier ground-breaking studies by Thomas.

3. In this book, we use the terms "learners" and "students" interchangeably. During the course of this study, learners/students within the literacy movement were exploring which of these terms would be most appropriate to describe their involvement in literacy programs.

4. The language experience story is widely used in adult literacy programs as a way of drawing upon learners' experiences to generate reading materials. In this method, the tutors act as scribes, writing down (without editing) what the learners say.

5.  Hope, Anne and Sally Timmel. *Training for Transformation: A Handbook for Community Workers.* Gweru, Zimbabwe: Mambo Press, 1984.

The notion of learners as "knowledge producers" is drawn from the work of Paulo Freire. Freire's theoretical work is popularized in this training manual.

6.  The Dolch reading list is a list of the most commonly used words in the English language, such as, "in", "the", "to", "go", and "from". Some believe that learning to read is facilitated when a learner memorizes this list.

7.  "Reading for meaning" refers to a way of teaching reading that stresses the importance of the readers understanding what they are reading. This is distinct from "reading phonetically," which stresses facility in the sound/letter correlation.

8.  Alden, Harold. *Illiteracy and Poverty in Canada: Toward a Critical Perspective.* Unpublished master's thesis, University of Toronto, Toronto, 1982, p.11-12.

9.  Booker, John et al. *ESL/Literacy: An Introductory Handbook for Tutors.* London: Adult Literacy and Basic Skills Unit, 1985, p.10-12.

10. Ontario Ministry of Education. *The Formative Years: Circular P1J1.* Toronto: Ontario Ministry of Education, 1975.

11. Source unknown.

12. Excerpt from "Bread and Roses" In Fowke, Edith and Joe Glazer. *Songs of Work and Protest.* New York: Dover Publications, 1973.

13. Hope, *op cit.*

NOTES

176

14. East End Literacy. *Annual Report 1984.* Toronto: East End Literacy, 1984, p.5.

15. Peel Literacy Guild. *Constitution and By-Laws.* Revised 06:88 Page 1 of the Constitution.

16. East End Literacy, *op cit,* p.4.

17. *Ibid.* p.29.

18. *Peel Literacy Guild Board Manual* 9/88, p.104.

# BIBLIOGRAPHY

Adult Literacy and Basic Skills Unit (ALBSU). *An Introduction to Literacy Teaching.* London: Adult Literacy and Basic Skills Unit, 1980.

Alcoff, Linda. "Cultural Feminism Versus Post-Structuralism: The Identity Crisis in Feminist Theory." *Signs* 13(31), 1988.

Alden, Harold. *Illiteracy and Poverty in Canada: Toward a Critical Perspective.* Unpublished master's thesis, University of Toronto, Toronto, 1982.

Alkenbrack, Betsy, et al. *Community-Based Literacy in an Urban Setting.* Toronto: Curriculum Working Group, 1984.

Arlen, Harold in David Bickman, ed. *The Harold Arlen Songbook.* United States: MPL Communications; Winona, MN; Milwaukee, WI. Exclusively distributed by Hal Leonard Pub. Corp., 1985.

Arnold, Rick, Deborah Barndt, and Bev Burke. *A New Weave: Popular Education in Canada and Central America.* Toronto: CUSO Development Education and Ontario Institute for Studies in Education, Adult Education Department, n.d.

Arnold, Rick and Bev Burke. *A Popular Education Handbook. An educational experience taken from Central America and adapted to the Canadian context.* Toronto: CUSO Development Education and Ontario Institute for Studies in Education, Adult Education Department, 1983.

Association for Community Based Education. *Adult Literacy: A Study of Community Based Literacy Programs. Volume I. Study Findings and Recommendations. Volume II. Program Profiles.* Washington, D.C.: Association for Community Based Education, 1986.

Atkinson, Tannis. *Speaking Our Own Voice.* Toronto: Adult Basic Education Unit, Toronto Board of Education, 1988.

Baum, Frank, with pictures by W.W. Denslow. *The Wizard of Oz.* Chicago: Rand McNally, 1956.

Bell, Jill and Barbara Burnaby. *A Handbook for ESL Literacy.* Toronto: OISE Press in association with Hodder & Stoughton Ltd., 1985.

Booker, John et al. *ESL/Literacy: An Introductory Handbook for Tutors.* London: Adult Literacy and Basic Skills Unit, 1985.

Brown, H. Douglas. *Principles of Language Learning and Teaching.* 2nd ed. New Jersey: Prentice-Hall, 1987.

Bruner, Jerome. *In Search of Mind: Essays in Autobiography.* New York: Harper and Row Publishers, 1983.

Canadian Congress for Learning Opportunities for Women (CCLOW). *Telling Our Stories Our Way: A Guide to Canadian Materials for Women Learning to Read.* Toronto: Canadian Congress for Learning Opportunities for Women, 1990.

Collie, Robert. *Getting Along.* Toronto: East End Literacy Press, 1986.

BIBLIOGRAPHY

Colvin, Ruth and Jane Root. *TUTOR*. New York: Literacy Volunteers of America, 1974.

Doiron, Rose. *My Name is Rose*. Toronto: East End Literacy Press, 1987.

Donald, James. "Language, Literacy and Schooling." England: Open University, Unit 29.

East End Literacy. *Annual Report*. Toronto: East End Literacy, 1984.

East End Literacy. *Let's Get Together*. Toronto: East End Literacy Press, 1987.

_____. *I Call It The Curse! A Book about Periods*. Toronto: East End Literacy Press, 1988.

_____. *Writer's Voice*. Toronto: East End Literacy Press, 1980-1988.

Fanon, Franz. *Black Skin, White Masks*. New York: Grove Press, 1967.

Fingeret, Arlene and Paul Jurmo, eds. "Participatory Literacy Education." *New Directions for Continuing Education Series, no. 42*. San Francisco: Jossey-Bass, 1989.

Fowke, Edith and Joe Glazer. *Songs of Work and Protest*. New York: Dover Publications, 1973.

Freire, Paulo. *Pedagogy of the Oppressed*. New York: Seabury Press, 1970.

Gaber-Katz, Elaine. "The Politics of Literacy: Educating for Continuity." In *Out of the Shadows*. Toronto: Ontario Educational Communications Authority, 1983.

Gaber-Katz, Elaine. *The Use of Story in Critical Literacy.*
Unpublished paper. Toronto, 1990.

Gaber-Katz, Elaine and Jennifer Horsman. "Is it her voice if she
speaks their words?" *Women and Literacy, Canadian Woman Studies*
9(3 & 4), 1988.

Gaber-Katz, Elaine and Gladys M. Watson. *Libraries for Literacy: The
1987 Toronto Public Library Literacy Report.* Toronto: Toronto
Public Library, 1987.

_____. "Community-based literacy programming – The Toronto
Experience." *Adult Literacy Perspectives.* James Draper and Maurice
Taylor (eds.) Toronto: Culture Concepts, 1989.

Garvie, Edie. *Story as Vehicle: Teaching English to Young Children.*
Cleveland, Avon, England: Multilingual Matters Ltd., 1990.

Gatt-Fly. *Ah-Hah! A New Approach to Popular Education.* Toronto:
Between the Lines, 1983.

Giroux, Henry. "Literacy, Critical Pedagogy, and Empowerment."
*Schooling and the Struggle for Public Life: Critical Pedagogy in the
Modern Age.* Minneapolis: University of Minnesota Press, 1988.

Good, Martin and John Holmes. *How's It Going? An Alternative to
Testing Students in Adult Literacy.* London: Adult Literacy and Basic
Skills Unit, 1982.

Goodman, Ken. *Language and Literacy: The Selected Writings of
Kenneth S. Goodman.* F. V. Gollash, ed. London: Routledge & Kegan
Paul, 1982.

Graves, Donald. *Writing: Teachers and Children at Work.* Portsmouth, New Hampshire: Heinemann Educational Books, 1983.

Greenspan, Miriam. *A New Approach to Women and Therapy.* New York; Toronto: McGraw Hill, 1983.

Guindon, Hank. *New Year's 1960.* Toronto: East End Literacy Press, 1985.

Hewitt, Priscilla. "Educating Priscilla." *Women and Literacy, Canadian Woman Studies* 9(3 & 4), 1988.

Hope, Anne and Sally Timmel. *Training for Transformation: A Handbook for Community Workers.* Book I, II, III. Zimbabwe: Mambo Press, 1986.

Horsman, Jennifer. "Discourses of Il/literacy: A Literature Review." *Women and Literacy, Canadian Woman Studies* 9(3 &4), 1988.

_____. *East End Literacy Evaluation.* Toronto: East End Literacy, 1982.

_____. *Something in My Mind Besides the Everyday: Women and Literacy.* Toronto: Women's Press, 1990.

Horsman, Jennifer, et al. *Lifeline to Literacy: People with Disabilities Speak Out.* Toronto: Ontario Educational Communications Authority, 1989.

Iaquinto, Margaret. *Reading and Writing Skills: A Kit for Tutors.* Australia: Council of Adult Education, 1983.

Knowles, Malcolm. *Self-directed Learning.* Chicago: Follett, 1975.

Krashen, Stephen D. *Inquiries & Insights: Second Language Teaching Immersion & Bilingual Education Literacy.* Hayward, California: Alemany Press, 1985.

Lee, Enid. *Letters to Marcia: A Teacher's Guide to Anti-Racist Education.* Toronto: Cross Cultural Communication Centre, 1985.

Mace, Jane. *Working with Words: Literacy Beyond School.* London: Writers and Readers Publishing Cooperative in Association with Chameleon, 1979.

Maguire, Paddy, et al. David Morley and Ken Worpole, eds. *The Republic of Letters: Working Class Writing and Local Publishing.* London: Comedia Publishing Group, 1982.

Marlatt, Daphne. "musing with mother tongue." *in the feminine: women and words conference proceedings.* Edmonton: University of Alberta, 1985.

McBeth, Sally and Vivian Stollmeyer. "East End Literacy: A Women's Discussion Group." *Women and Literacy, Canadian Woman Studies* 9(3 & 4), 1988.

Morton, Janet. *Assessing Vocational Readiness in Low Income Women: An Exploration into the Construction and Use of Ideology.* Unpublished master's thesis, University of Toronto, Toronto, 1985.

*Neighbours.* 1987-1988. Newsletter of the Davenport-Perth Neighbourhood Community Centre.

Nunan, David. *The Learner-Centred Curriculum.* Cambridge: Cambridge University Press, 1988.

BIBLIOGRAPHY

Ontario Ministry of Education. *The Formative Years: Circular P1J1.* Toronto: Ontario Ministry of Education, 1975.

*Opening Time.* Manchester: The Gatehouse Project, 1986.

Peel Literacy Guild. *Peel Literacy Guild Board Manual.*

_____. *Constitution and By-Laws.* Revised 06:88.

_____. *Words.* Toronto: Peel Literacy Guild, 1987-1988.

Pratt, Sydney. "Literacy: Charitable Enterprise or Political Right?" Toronto: St. Christopher House, 1980. Mimeograph.

Richards, Jack, and Theodore S Rogers. *Approaches and Methods in Language Teaching.* Cambridge: Cambridge University Press, 1986.

Rockhill, Kathleen. "The Other City . . . Where No One Reads." *Women and Literacy, Canadian Woman Studies* 9(3 & 4), 1988.

Rosen, Harold. "The Importance of Story." *Language Arts* 63(3), 1986.

Sheridan, Lee. *Raised Up Down South.* Toronto: East End Literacy Press, 1988.

Shor, Ira. *Critical Teaching and Everyday Life.* Montreal: Black Rose Books, 1980.

Simon, Roger. "Empowerment as a Pedagogy of Possibility." *Language Arts* 64(4), 1987.

Smith, Frank. *Reading without Nonsense.* New York: Teachers College Press, 1978.

_____. *Understanding Reading: A Psycholinguistic Analysis of Reading and Learning to Read.* New York: Holt, Rinehart and Winston, Inc., 1971.

Spender, Dale. *Man Made Language.* London: Kegan Paul, 1985.

Steedman, Carolyn. *Landscape for a Good Woman: A story of two lives.* London: Virago, 1986.

Students for Action. *Working Together.* Toronto: East End Literacy Press, 1985.

Thomas, Audrey. *Adult Illiteracy in Canada: A Challenge.* Canadian Commission for Unesco Occasional Paper no. 42. Ottawa: Canadian Commission for Unesco, Summer 1983.

Thomas, Barb. *Multiculturalism in the Workplace.* Toronto: YWCA of Metropolitan Toronto, 1986.

Trudgill, Peter. *Sociolinguistics: An Introduction to Language and Society.* England: Penguin Books, 1983.

Weedon, Chris. *Feminist Practice and Poststructuralist Theory.* Oxford: Blackwell, 1987.

Weiler, Kathleen. *Women Teaching for Change: Gender, Class & Power.* Massachusetts: Bergin & Garvey, 1988.

*Women and Literacy, Canadian Woman Studies* 9(3 & 4), 1988.

Women's Self Help Network. *Working Together for Change: Women's Self Help Network.* Campbell River, British Columbia: Ptarmigan Press, 1985.